THE PENGUIN BOOK OF EXOTIC WORDS

Janet Whitcut was Senior Research Editor of the Longman Dictionary and Reference Book Unit and is now a freelance writer with a special interest in language and lexicography. She has worked on a number of prestigious dictionaries, among them the *Longman Dictionary of the English Language* (1984), and is co-author of the *Little Oxford Guide to English Usage* (1994), *Mastering English Usage* (1994), *Usage and Abusage* (Penguin, 1995) and the *Longman Guide to English Usage* (Penguin, 1996).

D1495528

The Penguin Book of
EXOTIC WORDS

JANET WHITCUT

Happy Fathers day '97

*And no, these are
not Erotic words*

Love Jason Spike

PENGUIN BOOKS

PENGUIN BOOKS

Published by the Penguin Group
Penguin Books Ltd, 27 Wrights Lane, London w8 5tz, England
Penguin Books USA Inc., 375 Hudson Street, New York, New York 10014, USA
Penguin Books Australia Ltd, Ringwood, Victoria, Australia
Penguin Books Canada Ltd, 10 Alcorn Avenue, Toronto, Ontario, Canada m4v 3b2
Penguin Books (NZ) Ltd, 182–190 Wairau Road, Auckland 10, New Zealand

Penguin Books Ltd, Registered Offices: Harmondsworth, Middlesex, England

First published 1996
1 3 5 7 9 10 8 6 4 2

Typeset in Monotype Bembo and Gill Sans
Typeset by Rowland Phototypesetting Ltd, Bury St Edmunds, Suffolk
Printed in England by Clays Ltd, St Ives plc

CONTENTS

ACKNOWLEDGEMENTS

A great many of the quotations in this book come from the *Oxford English Dictionary* and the Oxford and Penguin dictionaries of quotations; some also from *Hobson-Jobson*, the Victorian glossary of 'Anglo-Indian' words. Of the rest, it seems unnecessary to recognize the involuntary contributions of Chaucer, for instance, or Dickens. But grateful acknowledgement is due to the following more recent authors: Douglas Adams, Woody Allen, Alan Bennett, Enid Blyton, Anthony Burgess, Alistair Cooke, Wendy Cope, Nigel Dennis, Monica Dickens, Michael Flanders, John Fowles, George MacDonald Fraser, Christopher Fry, Richard Hoggart, Michael Innes, John Le Carré, Tom Lehrer, Ruth Rendell, Tom Stoppard, Sue Townsend, Hugh Trevor-Roper, Angus Wilson, Philip Woodruff.

I am indebted to Cleodie MacKinnon for several helpful additions.

INTRODUCTION

English is by far the most important and widely used language in the world today. It is not the one with the greatest number of native speakers, because that is undoubtedly Chinese. But it is the *native* language, the mother tongue, of 300 million people, dispersed all over the world in politically and economically important countries. It is the *second* language – used within their own country – of many more. This is particularly so in India and Africa, even where English might be regarded as a symbol of past colonialism which it would be pleasant to get rid of: India, for instance, has 3,000 English newspapers, and uses English very largely in higher education. But one should not forget that English is also the second language of French speakers in Quebec, and of some native speakers of the Celtic languages. Finally, English is the chief *foreign* language, for international communication, of nearly everyone else.

It is the lingua franca of science and technology; of scholarship; of international travel; of aviation and shipping; of computers; of sport and pop music. There is everywhere an insatiable desire to learn it, so that probably more school timetable hours are devoted to it worldwide than to any other subject; understandably, since it is such a necessary requirement for good jobs. It is the chief working language of the UN, and the language of probably 60 per cent of the world's broadcasting and 70 per cent of its mail.

Many people have to learn English as a foreign language to talk to each other. In the Volkswagen factory in Shanghai, that is how the Germans and Chinese communicate. Even the French have had reluctantly to capitulate over this, though with bitter resentment. Their language, after all, held for two hundred years, until early this century, the position from which it has now been ousted by English. Today the prestigious French Pasteur Institute publishes its international medical journal in English. General de Gaulle was distressed to find that computers talk English, not French.

Even where people speak their own language, that language may be increasingly besprinkled with English words. Some are truly international today: airport, passport, hotel, telephone, bar, soda, cigarette, sport, golf, tennis, weekend, jeans, know-how, sex appeal, no problem, OK. French has un pyjama, le gadget, le jerrycan, le self-service, le do-it-yourself, le pipeline, le chewing-gum, le cameraman, les refuelling stops. The Germans speak of das Cash-flow, die Teenagers, die Shorts, das Walkout; the Spanish of streptease, and the Italians of il software; the Russians of basketball and trolleybus; the Poles of slums, komiks, telewizja; the Japanese of a nekutai (necktie) and an erebeta (elevator). Malaysian has komprehensif and eksperimen, and the West African language Hausa has sukurudireba (screwdriver).

Intriguingly, other languages are also well provided with apparently 'English' words that have gone a bit wrong, and do not actually exist in English. The French have a 'pull' for a sweater, 'footing' for walking or jogging, a 'smoking' for a dinner-jacket, a 'self' for a self-service restaurant. In Czech, 'nonstop' means round-the-clock, which sounds odd in the context of 'nonstop parking'. In Serbo-Croat 'nylon' means something like disreputable, so that a 'nylon hotel' is a brothel. Japanese has the word 'salaryman', for a middle-management white-collar worker, and uses 'veteran' for expert. And in Indian English a 'troubleshooter' apparently makes trouble rather than dealing with it.

Some words in the English-based 'mixed' languages, pidgin and creole, might certainly be regarded as examples of 'English gone wrong'. 'Bikbik' means 'very big' in many pidgins and creoles; 'grass' may mean hair or feathers, and 'plenti han' (from plenty + hand) a centipede. But it is probably more accurate to call these languages legitimate varieties of English in their own right.

Samuel Daniel prophesied the spread of English in his *Musophilus* (1599):

> And who in time knows whither we may vent
> The treasure of our tongue, to what strange shores
> This gain of our best glory shall be sent,
> T'enrich unknowing Nations with our stores?

Despite its overriding importance in the world, it would be meaningless to claim that English is the 'best' language. What it does have is an unusually rich vocabulary; it has been said that English is the only language that has, or needs, dictionaries of synonyms such as *Roget's Thesaurus*. It has always freely admitted new words whenever it needed them. For instance, we learned a lot about music from Italy, and our musical words – soprano, diminuendo – are still Italian. As Evelyn wrote in his *Memoirs* (1667): 'We have hardly any words that do so fully express the French ... naïvety, ennui, bizarre, concert ... emotion, defer, effort ... let us therefore (as the Romans did the Greek) make as many of these do homage as are likely to prove good citizens.' And Dr Johnson wrote in the next century: 'Words are seldom synonimus; a new term was not introduced, but because the former was thought inadequate.' Johnson was fairly happy about this, accepting that the language has been 'suffered to spread, under the direction of chance, into wild exuberance'; although he did feel it his duty to 'warn others against the folly of naturalizing useless foreigners to the injury of the natives'.

Just as today some English people inveigh against incoming Americanisms – cohort for 'companion', normalcy for 'normality' – so there have always been some people to resist incoming foreignisms. In 1553 Thomas Wilson wrote: 'Some farre journeyed gentlemen at their returne home, like as they loue to goe in forraine apparelle, so thei will pouder their talke with ouersea language.' That is the kind of thing Shakespeare is laughing at Tybalt for in *Romeo and Juliet*: 'ah, the immortal passado! the punto reverso! the hai!'

But unlike French, English has never had an Academy to control its 'exuberance'. Johnson took a sturdily British line about that: 'If an academy should be established for the cultivation of our stile, which I, who can never wish to see dependance multiplied, hope the spirit of English liberty will hinder or destroy . . .' In any case, he realized very well that such efforts are doomed to failure: 'Academies have been instituted, to guard the avenues of their languages, to retain fugitives, and repulse intruders; but their vigilance and activity have hitherto been vain; sounds are too volatile and subtile for legal restraints; to enchain syllables, and to lash the wind, are equally the undertakings of pride, unwilling to measure its desires by its strength.'

So where do all the words come from? The common core of English is Germanic. The Germanic languages are a branch of the great Indo-European family, to which belong the languages of most of Europe and of Iran, India, and some other parts of Asia. In the fifth and sixth centuries the Angles, Saxons, and Jutes, West Germanic tribes, invaded Britain, driving the Celtic-speaking population north and west. (There are few Celtic words in modern English, apart from place-names. Those that we have – Tory, whisky – came in later.) Some of our most basic words – house, man, bread, speak – are Saxon. The conversion of Britain to Christianity brought an influx of religious words – abbot, priest, mass, altar; and of the vocabulary of education and learning – school, verse, grammar. Then in the ninth and tenth centuries came the invasion of the Vikings, who brought Norse words – law, egg, sister, sky. From the eleventh century onwards, after the Norman Conquest, there came a flood of French words, conspicuously in the field of law and government – judge, court, country; in the army – soldier, captain; and in the nobility – duke, baron. And English continued to be assailed by new words from the learned languages, Latin, Greek, and Hebrew. As one Richard Verstegan complained in *A Restitution of Decayed Intelligence* (1605): 'As well might we fetch words from the *Ethiopians*, or East or West *Indians*, and thrust them into our Language, and baptize all by the name of *English*, as those which we daily take from the *Latine* or languages thereon depending.'

And, of course, we have indeed 'fetched words from the East or West Indians': curry from Tamil, canoe from Arawakan. English has long been a language of traders, explorers, and settlers, and the words those people encountered all over the world have flowed freely into this central sea. These are usually the names of new 'things' which they found on their travels in the Old or New World, and called by their native names: chocolate (Aztec), chimpanzee (Kongo), rickshaw (Japanese). It is particularly noticeable how many English words come from the Indian subcontinent – polo, bungalow, chutney, pyjamas. This is natural enough. The British Raj lasted almost three hundred years, and India was for a long time the most important and influential part of the former British Empire. Moreover, it was a part of the empire from which the British *returned*, unlike the colonists of Canada, Australia, and New Zealand, bringing their words home with them.

In this book I have assembled a bouquet of words that have passed into English from many interesting or unexpected sources, with examples of their use – famous, original, or merely funny. They have all given me pleasure as a working lexicographer.

PEOPLE, I

First come some people of prestigious status:

A **mogul**, in the sense of an important person such as the head of a film studio, traces his descent from the Persian *muğūl*. This means either a Mongol (in 1298 Marco Polo referred to '"Mungul", a name sometimes applied to the Tartars') or a member of the Muslim dynasty of Mughals in India from the sixteenth to the nineteenth century. These were descendants of Tamerlane, and ruled from Delhi over most of India. The last emperor was dethroned in 1857, after the Mutiny. The Moguls or Mughals constituted a distinct Muslim caste in India. In 1781 somebody was advertising in the *India Gazette* for 'an European or Mogul Coachman that can drive four Horses in hand'. The spellings Mogul and Mughal seem to be preferred today with reference to the Indian art of the Mogul empire.

A **tycoon**, rather the same sort of person as a mogul, gets his name from the Japanese *taikun*, 'great lord'. The title was used (apparently incorrectly) by foreigners in the nineteenth century with reference to the shogun of Japan, the hereditary commander-in-chief. The word caught on first in American use, with the meaning of a business or political magnate: it was used at the time of the American Civil War as a nickname of Abraham Lincoln. In 1960, by the way, the *Guardian* created a feminine form: 'A high-powered tycooness must have sharp claws within the velvet paw.'

A **mandarin** is also a person of oriental origin, deriving his name through Portuguese, Malay, and Hindi from *mantrin*, the Sanskrit word for 'counsellor'. Historically the mandarins of China were officials of the civil service, referred to in English under that name from the sixteenth century. (Mandarin is also the official language of modern China.) In modern use a mandarin is likely to be a senior bureaucrat, or a member of the literary establishment. As an adjective it has come to mean 'highbrow', and to be somewhat abusive. In *Mr Britling Sees It Through* (1916) H. G. Wells referred to 'the conservative classes whose education has always had a mandarin quality – very, very little of it, and very old and choice'. In *Enemies of Promise* (1938) Cyril Connolly wrote, 'I have called this style the Mandarin style, since it is beloved by literary pundits, by those who would make the written word as unlike as possible to the spoken one.'

A **nabob** also started life in the East. The older form is **nawab**, from the Urdu *nawab*, the title of a local governor or nobleman in India in the past or in Pakistan today. But the word nabob was used in eighteenth-century England for anyone, from Clive onwards, who had returned from India – having successfully 'shaken the pagoda-tree' as they said – with a large fortune. Nabobs were somewhat looked down on as *nouveaux riches*, but courted for their enormous wealth. Boswell recorded in his *Journal of a Tour to the Hebrides* (1773) Dr Johnson's sardonic comment: 'Why, sir, the Nabob will carry it [an election] by means of his wealth, in a country where money is highly valued, as it must be where nothing can be had without money; but if it comes to personal preference, the man of family will always carry it.' In 1840 Macaulay described Clive as 'A savage old Nabob, with an immense fortune, a tawny complexion, a bad liver, and a worse heart.'

With **boss** we move further west. This word began life as early as the seventeenth century in America, from the Dutch word *baas*, 'master'. (The Dutch form is still current in South African English.) By 1868 Walt Whitman was writing, for instance, in *To Working Men*: 'Were I to you as the boss employing and paying you, would that satisfy you?' Whitman's egalitarian audience would not have let the servile word 'master' pass their lips. By the late nineteenth century it came also to mean the head of an American political party machine, a professional politician controlling a lot of votes.

'Boss' seems to have become current in Britain only in this century. Shaw wrote in his Preface to *The Millionairess* (1936): 'A born boss is one who rides roughshod over us by some mysterious power that separates him from our species and makes us fear him.' And in *The Road to Wigan Pier* (1937) Orwell referred to 'the accent and manners which stamp you as one of the boss class'.

lord and **lady** are of course very ancient, Old English in fact; but it is interesting that both of them are to do with bread. A lord is a *hlāfweard*, 'bread-keeper', like Loaf Ward. A lady is a *hlāefdige*, 'loaf-kneader'.

panjandrum was invented, by the English playwright and actor Samuel Foote, in 1765, as part of a nonsense story of *non sequiturs*, to test the memory of someone who claimed to be able to repeat anything after once hearing it. The relevant bit runs: 'and there were present the Picninnies, and the Joblillies, and the Garyulies, and the great Panjandrum himself, with the little round button on top'. The Victorian illustrator Randolph Caldecott depicts this distinguished personage as a rubicund old gentleman in full academicals, clutching a Latin grammar in one hand and a birch rod for flogging in the other. The word seems to have caught various people's fancy as a burlesque title for someone both powerful and pompous. In 1900 the *Pall Mall Gazette* commented, '. . . so will the great British public, even though it may scarcely know what sort of a Panjandrum a Senior Wrangler is'.

pontiff is about the most prestigious title of all, since there is only one of him. He is the Pope. It comes from *pontifex*, a priest of ancient Rome, and that in its turn comes from *pons*, 'a bridge', and *facere*, 'to make'. The bridges over the Tiber were apparently in the particular care of the principal college of priests. Longfellow wrote piously in *The Golden Legend* (1872):

> Well has the name of Pontifex been given
> Unto the church's head, as the chief builder
> And architect of the invisible bridge
> That leads from earth to heaven.

3

This mystical interpretation, though, has not much to do with the original meaning of the word.

And now some people in more subordinate positions:

A **secretary** was originally somebody who knew one's secrets, a confidant. In his *Compleat Angler* (1653) Izaak Walton refers to 'the great Secretary of Nature and all learning, Sir Francis Bacon', meaning that Bacon knew Nature's secrets. The word soon came to mean somebody who conducts somebody else's correspondence and does various sorts of office work, which is its most familiar sense today; but in the titles of various civil service and parliamentary posts, it perhaps retains something of the older sense of confidentiality.

A **secretary bird** is of course not an office girl but an African bird, so called from its feathery crest, which looks like a bunch of quill pens stuck behind someone's ear. No doubt secretaries who used quills did need a whole lot of them, because they had to be constantly repaired; that was what penknives were for. In *Mansfield Park* Jane Austen describes a pleasing scene where the big boy helps the little girl to write a letter, 'to assist her with his penknife or his orthography, as either were wanted'.

A **caddie** was originally Scottish. (So, of course, is the game of golf with which he or she is nowadays associated.) In Scots English, the word is a version of *cadet*, which meant a younger son or brother, or a young gentleman in the army. In eighteenth-century Edinburgh, caddies were odd-job men who acted as porters and messenger boys. The spelling of the word took a long time to settle down (cawdy, cadie, etc.) and it still sometimes takes the form of **caddy**, which properly speaking is a box or tin for tea, and is not Scottish at all but Malay: *kātī*, 'a one-and-a-third lb weight'. It seems that at one time Harley Street in London was known as 'the tea caddy', because so many directors of the East India Company lived there.

More interestingly, caddie was early shortened to **cad**, who in nineteenth-century England was a conductor on an omnibus. In *Pickwick Papers* (1837) Dickens refers to 'numerous cads and drivers of short stages', and in his *Book of Snobs* (1848) Thackeray speaks of 'a sceptical audience of omnibus-cads and nursemaids'. George MacDonald Fraser, impeccable as ever in matters of historical detail, picks up this sense in *Royal Flash* (1970): 'On the way to the club Speed was taken with the notion of boarding one of the new buses; he wanted to argue with the cad about the fare and provoke him into swearing; the bus cads were quite famous for their filthy language, and Speed reckoned it would be fun to have him get in a bate and horrify the passengers.'

Thereafter, the word came down in the world. From being a kind of low fellow who hung about the place hoping for work, a cad came to be a town lad at Oxford, sneered at as vulgar by the undergraduates, as in Clough's poem (1850):

> And if I should chance to run over a cad
> I can pay for the damage if ever so bad.
> So pleasant it is to have money, heigh ho . . .

and hence to mean anyone who behaves offensively and dishonourably.

pal also started life rather discreditably. In the Gypsy language, Romany, it means 'brother' or 'mate'; though a woman can be a pal too. But it often also meant a criminal accomplice. In 1789 someone explained that 'when highwaymen rob in pairs, they say such a one was his or my pal'.

Another word for 'mate' is **companion**, originally a messmate, someone you ate with: Latin *com*-, 'together', + *panis*, 'bread'. So a **company** ought to be a group of companions. Both words have existed in English since the thirteenth century. Companions were among other things the members, now only the lowest members, of an order of knighthood, as in Companion of the Order of St Michael and St George (CMG). Company can be anyone who prevents one from being alone; as when Pope in his *Essay on Man* (1732) writes of the simple Indian's hope of heaven, who

> thinks, admitted to that equal sky,
> His faithful dog shall bear him company.

Already by the fourteenth century a company could mean a medieval trade guild, as with the London City companies. When merchants began to collaborate to share the costs and risks of foreign adventuring, they became joint-stock companies, or corporations, such as the British East India Company. (The latter was nicknamed 'John Company', originally to impress Indians who could only imagine trading with a single potentate.)

coolie is an Indian word of disputed origin. It may come from the Tamil word *kulī*, 'a hireling', or else from the name of an aboriginal tribe of Gujerat, 'formerly noted,' as the *Oxford English Dictionary* comments, 'as robbers, but now settling down as respectable labourers and cultivators'. Whatever its origin, the word came to be used particularly of unskilled labourers from India or China imported into foreign countries, often in conditions very near to slavery. They worked in the plantations, and built the great transcontinental American railroads. In his *America* (1974) Alistair Cooke explains that there were two railroad companies, the Union Pacific in the East and the Central Pacific in the West, who in the 1860s raced to meet somewhere in the middle. (They finally met in Utah.) 'Whereas the Eastern gangs were recruited from immigrant Irish, from the defeated Southern whites, and blacks, the Western crew came mostly from China. The Union Pacific, it was said, was sustained by whiskey, the Central Pacific by tea.' These tea drinkers were coolies.

pawn comes ultimately from the Latin *pedo*, 'foot-soldier', from *pes*, 'foot'. Today we think of it chiefly as the smallest and most numerous piece in chess, but when it means somebody used by others for their own purposes, it comes perhaps closer to the root meaning. The chess sense occurs in Chaucer (1369): 'Mate in the myd poynt of the chekkere/ With a poune errante'.

The word has nothing to do with pawning things at a pawnbroker's. But it has the same Latin root as **peon**, which reached us through Portuguese and Spanish. In the Indian subcontinent, where the word came through Portuguese, a peon was first a foot-soldier, and now today is an orderly or messenger in a modern office. In South America, where it came from Spanish, a peon is a day labourer or a farm worker. Since this American sense is probably the more familiar one today, a visitor to India may be puzzled by remarks such as 'I'll send my peon over with the list.'

A **pariah**, a social outcast, gets his name from Tamil. In south India a numerous caste were the hereditary drummers, the *paṛaiyar*, who beat the big drum at festivals. They were despised for drunkenness and for eating forbidden meat, and were strictly avoided by orthodox Hindus. In 1787 a Colonel Fullarton wrote, 'I cannot persuade myself that it is judicious to admit Parias into battalions with men of respectable castes', and one of the obstacles to the progress of Christianity in India was the admission of these people into the churches.

The word came to have a pretty general application. In 1901 one journal commented, 'Ibsen is the supreme pariah of the English stage.'

boy is now quite rightly disapproved of as the word for a non-White male servant. In 1963 the Johannesburg City Council banned its use to refer to its African employees. Tom Stoppard made the point ironically in his play *Night and Day*: 'By the way, we don't call them boy any more. The idea is, if we don't call them boy they won't chop us with their machetes.'

However, 'boy' in this sense may not have started life as an English word at all. There was a south Indian caste of palanquin-bearers called *bhoi* or *boyi* in Tamil, Telugu, and Malayalam, and the Portuguese and French were using the word in their own languages in that sense, in parts of India that the English language had not yet reached.

A **slave** was originally an ethnic Slav. The Greek word *Sklabos*, for those peoples of central Europe, had come by as early as the ninth century to mean a person who is the property of another, since large numbers of Slavs had been reduced to slavery in the period of the Roman Empire. How Slavs became slaves is illustrated by a letter from a fourth-century Roman senator, who asked a crony on the Danube to buy him twenty slave boys, 'because on the frontier it is easy to find slaves and the price is usually tolerable'.

By the fourteenth century Chaucer's Troilus was using the word in English as we do. Grateful to Pandarus for organizing his love affair with Criseyde so nicely, he exclaimed: 'I can no more, but that I wol thee serve/ Right as thy sclave . . .' In technological use a 'slave' can be a thing: a subsidiary device directly controlled by another.

The **rank and file** – ordinary people – were originally ordinary soldiers: corporals and privates. A rank of soldiers is drawn up abreast, a file is one behind the other; so the two together, as defined in a military dictionary of 1802, are 'the horizontal and vertical lines of soldiers when drawn up for service'. The two ideas are nicely distinguished in chess, where a rank is a row of squares across the board from side to side, and a file is a line of squares from one player to the other.

Here are a few more professions and occupations, creditable and otherwise.

A **mountebank** climbed up on benches: Italian *monta in banco*. From this elevation he entertained his public with tricks and juggling, and dispensed quack medicines. In his *Advancement of Learning* (1605) Bacon complained that 'Men . . . will often preferre a Mountabanke or Witch, before a learned Phisitian.' Joseph Addison in *The Tatler* (1709) recounted, 'I remember when our whole island was shaken with an earthquake some years ago, there was an impudent mountebank who sold pills which (as he told the country people) were very good against an earthquake.'

It was an easy step to the more general sense of a showy charlatan. In 1852 Gladstone inveighed against 'theatrical, not to say charlatan and mountebank, politics'.

An **acrobat** was said to walk on tiptoe: Greek *akron*, 'summit', + *baino*, 'walk'. The word existed in ancient Greek, and seems to have meant a person who danced on ropes, though no doubt they did other tricks, such as turning somersaults. But the word has long been used, rather disparagingly, of people renowned for mental agility in changing their minds.

A **navvy** was a 'navigator', and his job at first was excavating canals; in the great period of their eighteenth-century construction the canals were called navigations. (It seems that the great engineer James Brindley, who laid out over 360 miles of canals all over the Midlands, had so little formal education that he spelt navvy like that.) When the railway age followed, great mobile teams of navvies moved about the country wherever they were needed, famous both for their prodigious vigour and for their enormous appetites. In 1846 Lord Stanley commented, 'The railway navigators . . . consume on an average two pounds of meat daily.'

They had a great reputation for drunkenness and violence. One of Robert Stephenson's assistant engineers reported,

These banditti, known in some parts of England by the name of 'Navies' or 'navigators' . . . are generally the terror of the surrounding country; they are as completely a class by themselves as the Gipsies. Possessed of all the daring recklessness of the Smuggler, without any of his redeeming qualities, their ferocious behaviour can only be equalled by the brutality of their language. It may be truly said, their hand is against every man, and before they have been long located, every man's hand is against them.

hussar is perhaps the most interesting of the many words for various kinds of soldiers. It comes through the Hungarian *huszár*, which first meant a Hungarian pirate or robber, and was an adaptation of the Italian *corsaro*, 'pirate, corsair'. By the fifteenth century a hussar was a Hungarian light cavalryman, and other nations including Britain formed hussar regiments. These regiments imitated the uniform of their Hungarian originals, part of which was the furry busby. In 1688 the *London Gazette* described a Bavarian hussar regiment as 'cloathed in Red, having Caps with Feathers on their Heads, and Wolfs Skins on their left Shoulders'. There were British hussars at Waterloo.

Hussars fought in a loose irregular manner. In *Tristram Shandy* (1762) Sterne describes some scribbled additions to a parson's funeral sermon: 'These, though hussar-like they skirmish lightly and out of all order, are still auxiliaries on the side of virtue.'

While we are on these military matters, **colonel** comes from the Italian *colonna*, 'column'. This is not of course the architectural sort of column, but an arrangement of troops who were led by this officer at the head of the regiment. The English word has existed since the sixteenth century, but only much more recently has begun to be pronounced like 'kernel'. This is shown by a rhyme (1691) from the works of Defoe – one can often deduce earlier pronunciations from rhymes:

> For equal Falshood, equal Fate befell,
> This dub'd a Knight, and that a Collonel.

An **admiral** is essentially the same person as an *amir*, or 'emir' (as in the United Arab Emirates of the Gulf). This Arabic word means 'commander'. It was usually followed by *al*, the Arabic 'the', to say what he was a commander of, and then there might be a word for 'sea' or 'water': an *amir-al-ma* was a commander of the sea under the caliph or sultan. The word came to be used in the British navy in the fourteenth century under Edward III, for the naval commander-in-chief or for various high-ranking naval officers. Somewhere along the way, it got itself mixed up with 'admirable'.

A **lieutenant** was originally somebody's deputy: French *lieu*, 'place', + *tenant*, 'holding'. The English word is quite old in that sense; in the fourteenth century the Archbishop of Canterbury was described as 'leeftenaunt of the pope'. In the army and navy, lieutenants are always next in rank below somebody – in the army below a captain. A lieutenant-commander, for instance, comes next below a commander.

An **amazon**, according to the Greeks, was *a*, 'without', + *mazos*, 'breast'. The idea was that this mythical tribe of female warriors amputated their right breasts, so as not to impede the drawing of the bow. They were said to live in Scythia, west of the Black Sea. Their babies were born as the result of annual visits to a neighbouring tribe, but the boy babies were either killed at birth or sent back to their fathers. According to Herodotus, the nearby Scythians proposed marriage at one time, but the Amazons said, 'We and the women of your nation could never live together; our ways are too much at variance. We are riders: our business is with the bow and the spear, and we know nothing of women's work.' (Yet the hero Theseus did marry the Amazon Queen Hippolyta, as Shakespeare recounts in *A Midsummer Night's Dream*.)

The Amazon river gets its name because in 1541 the Spanish explorer Orellana claimed to have met some female warriors there.

A **cavalier** ought properly to be mounted on horseback: from Latin *caballus*, 'horse'. From being a gentleman horse-soldier a cavalier came to be simply a court gentleman, and particularly one who was gallant with the ladies. The term Cavalier, for the supporters of Charles I in the Civil War, was first applied as a term of reproach by the other side. They meant by it a sort of swaggering warmonger. Those Cavaliers were identified by Sellar and Yeatman in *1066 and All That* (1930) as 'Wrong but Wromantic' while the Roundheads were 'Right but Repulsive'.

But the word has generally been used appreciatively. Burke in his *Reflections on the Revolution in France* (1790) commented: 'Little did I dream that I should have lived to see disasters fallen upon [the Queen of France] in a nation of gallant men, in a nation of men of honour, and of cavaliers.'

Today, a **civil engineer** designs roads, railways, bridges, dams, and so on, in contrast to mechanical, electrical, chemical, and no doubt several other kinds of engineer. But 'civil' is a confusing sort of word. It can mean 'polite' – which an engineer may or may not be; or 'between fellow-citizens', as with a Civil War; or 'about the private rights of individuals', as with the civil law. However, an important meaning of 'civil' is a negative one: 'not military or naval'. Civil engineers began to be distinguished, in the eighteenth century, from the division of the army who designed military works. It is recorded that 'The first meeting of this new institution, the Society of civil engineers, was held on the 15th of April 1793.'

But any kind of **engineer** ought to be 'ingenious'. The Latin *ingenium* means 'cleverness', and an engine is something that has been cleverly invented. Engineers, from the fifteenth century, were people who invented or designed things, and later those who constructed military works. The engineer in *Hamlet* who was to be 'hoist with his own petar' was going to be blown up (hoist) by a mine (petar) that he had put there himself to undermine a fortification. A sort of own goal.

In America, the word is used for the driver of a railway engine, as with Casey Jones, the hero of the ballad:

> Come all you rounders if you want to hear
> The story of a brave engineer,
> Casey Jones was the rounder's name,
> On a six eight-wheeler, boys, he won his fame . . .

To 'engineer' an enterprise may mean to superintend or contrive or manoeuvre it. Thus, 'social engineering' now means the application of sociological principles to social problems.

A **butler** is, properly speaking, in charge of bottles. The name of his job comes from the Old French *bouteillier*. The word was used in English, by the thirteenth century, for the butler who was sacked by Pharaoh but reassured by Joseph that he would be reinstated. He was in fact Pharaoh's cupbearer. More recently, though, the butler was the responsible servant of a considerable household, in charge not only of the cellar but of the plate.

Some of the best butlers in modern literature are chronicled by P. G. Wodehouse (Jeeves wasn't a butler, but a valet, or 'gentleman's personal gentleman'): 'Vintage butlers who weighed two hundred and fifty pounds on the hoof, butlers with three chins and bulging abdomens, butlers with that austere, supercilious butlerine manner which has passed away so completely. Butlers had been butlers then, in the deepest and holiest sense of the word.'

A **plumber** used formerly to work with lead pipes: Latin *plumbum*, 'lead'. Since lead is heavy it has been used at the end of plumb-lines to measure the depth of water, or to establish a vertical line. So to 'plumb' anything is not necessarily to install plumbing; it often means to measure its depth, literally or metaphorically. Gulliver in Swift's *Gulliver's Travels* (1726) 'consulted the most experienced seamen upon the depth of the channel, which they had often plummed', before his expedition to capture the fleet of the enemies of Lilliput.

Plumbers once did any work that involved lead, such as medieval church roofs – rather different from the occupation of the skilled craftsman that Woody Allen wanted in 1969: 'Not only is there no God, but try getting a plumber on weekends.'

The **haberdasher** has a mysterious origin. He may come from *hapertas*, the medieval Anglo-French name of an imported fabric. The word has existed in English for a long time: 'an Haberdasshere' was one of the more prosperous pilgrims in Chaucer's *Canterbury Tales* (*c.* 1386), though he never gets as far as telling a story. They sold all sorts of small articles; a list from 1561 pleasingly lists 'mousetrappes, bird cages, shooing hornes, Lanthornes, and Jews trumpes'.

When Lord Peter Wimsey's manservant in Dorothy L. Sayers's *Strong Poison* (1930) suspects that his master is contemplating matrimony, he comments, 'I had thought it possible that, if your lordship was about to contract new ties –' to be answered, 'I *knew* it was something in the haberdashery line!'

An **umpire** – like an adder (q.v.) – was once a numpire. The Old French word *nonper* means 'not equal', like 'non' + 'peer'. But this word for an impartial arbitrator between disputants had taken the form in which we know it by the fifteenth century, and was much used in legal contexts. Today, though, we think of it mostly in connection with sports; as in Andrew Lang's *Brahma*, in imitation of Emerson:

> If the wild bowler thinks he bowls,
> Or if the batsman thinks he's bowled,
> They know not, poor misguided souls,
> They too shall perish unconsoled.
> *I* am the batsman and the bat,
> *I* am the bowler and the ball,
> The umpire, the pavilion cat,
> The roller, pitch, and stumps, and all.

The first **martinet** was the Marquis de *Martinet*, a seventeenth-century drill-master and lieutenant-colonel in Louis XIV's army. He was killed at the siege of Duisberg by what would now be called 'friendly fire'. The strictness of his discipline in military drill preserved his name to be given, usually disparagingly, to any rigid disciplinarian.

A **buccaneer** is decidedly a person of the New World. *Boucan* is the French spelling of a word in Tupi, a language of the Amazon, and it means a framework for barbecueing meat over a fire, or smoking it to preserve it. The French hunters in those parts who cured their meat in the Indian manner were called buccaneers, and the word came to be used for the pirates who ravaged the Spanish-American coast. It then came to mean piratical sea-rovers in general, as when Defoe (1703) speaks of 'buccaneering Danes'; then by extension any unscrupulous adventurer by sea or land. In 1883 the *Glasgow Weekly Herald* referred to Garibaldi as 'that glorious old buccaneer'.

A **thug** was originally a member of an Indian religious group of professional robbers and stranglers, dedicated to the goddess Kali, who attacked travellers on the roads. It took most of the nineteenth century to suppress them. The word comes from the Hindi and Marathi *ṭhag*, 'swindler'. It came later to be used of violent ruffians or hired gangsters in general, and was applied, for instance, to Hitler's Brown-shirts.

An **assassin**, an equally violent person, is also of oriental origin. This word comes from the Arabic *ḥaššāš*, 'hashish-eater'. It seems always to have been applied to someone – such as Brutus and his fellow conspirators in *Julius Caesar* or John Wilkes Booth who shot Abraham Lincoln – who kills an important public figure, and it goes back to the time of the Crusades. There was a group of Muslim fanatics who intoxicated themselves with hashish before setting forth to murder the Christian leaders. It can of course be used metaphorically, as when the *Guardian* in 1962 referred to 'helping the Prime Minister in his political battle to assassinate Mr George Brown'.

The Russian Constitution has been defined as 'absolutism tempered by assassination'.

A **vandal** was originally a member of a wild Germanic tribe called the *Vandals*, who in the fourth and fifth centuries ravaged

Gaul, Spain, and north Africa, and sacked Rome in 455. They gained an unfortunate reputation for destroying books and works of art, which is why the word is now used when people vandalize telephone boxes.

A **scapegoat** was originally an actual goat, not a person. The word seems to have been invented in 1530 by William Tyndale for his English translation of the Bible. It translates the Hebrew word used in the sixteenth chapter of Leviticus, where God instructs Moses that two goats are to be sacrificed. The priest Aaron is to cast lots between the goats; one is to be killed as a sin offering, the other to be driven alive into the desert: 'And Aaron shall lay both his hands upon the head of the live goat, and confess over him all the iniquities of the children of Israel . . . And the goat shall bear upon him all their iniquities unto a land not inhabited: and he shall let go the goat in the wilderness.'

In 1856 the Pre-Raphaelite painter Holman Hunt actually went to the Dead Sea to give verisimilitude to his famous work 'The Scapegoat'; and in his poem 'In the Wilderness' Robert Graves nicely compares the roles of the goat and Jesus:

> Ever with him went,
> Of all his wanderings
> Comrade, with ragged coat,
> Gaunt ribs – poor innocent –
> Bleeding foot, burning throat,
> The guileless young scapegoat . . .

A **catamite** is a boy kept by a pederast (or 'kept for unnatural purposes', as the sober old *Oxford English Dictionary* has it), and the word has a distinguished classical origin. It comes from the name of *Ganymede*, the young cupbearer of the Greek god Zeus who was taken up to Olympus for his beauty. Perhaps this was never a very common word, but in the freer atmosphere of today it is now mentionable. As Anthony Burgess recounts in *Earthly Powers* (1980): 'It was the afternoon of my eighty-first birthday, and I was in bed with my catamite when Ali announced that the archbishop had come to see me.'

cannibal (if this can be called an occupation) comes through Spanish from *Carib*, the name of a tribe of the West Indies and nearby coasts, who were reported to eat people. When Columbus reached the West Indies he heard this name in its Spanish form *Canibales*, and reported 'The natives live in great fear of the canibals.' The word was known in that form in sixteenth-century English; a variant is Caliban, the name of Shakespeare's wild man in *The Tempest*, though there is no suggestion that he ever ate anyone. But Shakespeare also knew the word in the form we have it today: Othello told Desdemona stories about

> the Cannibals that each other eat,
> The Anthropophagi, and men whose heads
> Do grow beneath their shoulders.

In *Moby Dick* (1851) Herman Melville uses the word to mean simply an alarming black person. At the Spouter-Inn, Ishmael is constrained to share a bed with the harpooner Queequeg from the South Seas: 'this wild cannibal, tomahawk between his teeth, sprang into bed with me'. But he concludes philosophically: 'Better sleep with a sober cannibal than a drunken Christian.'

A **bastard**, it seems, was begotten on a mule's pack-saddle, rather than properly in bed. The saddle was a *bast* in Old French, and the muleteers slept on them at inns.

We have had the word in English since the early Middle Ages, and Shakespeare makes some play with it in *King Lear*. The Earl of Gloucester's bastard son Edmund soliloquizes:

> Edmund the base
> Shall top the legitimate. I grow, I prosper.
> Now, gods, stand up for bastards!

It is odd that when the word is used figuratively a bastard is a disagreeable person or thing, but with an adjective it can sound quite friendly: 'You lucky bastard!'

A **bugger** was originally a Bulgarian, from the medieval Latin *Bulgarus*. As members of the Greek Church, Bulgarians were denounced as heretics, which suggested that they must be guilty of all sorts of abominable practices, sodomy among them.

As with bastard, the word used with an adjective is quite friendly, though no doubt coarse: 'You clever bugger!' And, in British use at least, the verb has become very popular. A character in Angus Wilson's *The Old Men at the Zoo* (1961) discusses a possible National Zoological Park, with 'hippos in their natural lovely setting of the Severn or beavers buggering up the Broads'. Nor should one forget King George V's reputed last words on his deathbed: 'Bugger Bognor.'

The rather slangy **berk** meaning 'fool' is a piece of rhyming slang. The sequence is cunt = Berkeley (or Berkshire) Hunt = *Berk*eley. In spite of its origin, this too seems to be quite a friendly thing to call anyone.

cabal comes ultimately from the Hebrew *cabbala*, the Jewish mystical interpretation of the Old Testament. Since this was an esoteric oral tradition, the word came to be used for a secret intrigue, or a small clique of people engaged in one. Then, by accident, the initial letters of the names of five of Charles II's ministers happened to form the word CABAL: Clifford, Arlington, Buckingham, Ashley, Lauderdale. This Cabal formed a small group within the Privy Council, a precursor of the modern Cabinet. They were thought of as too influential, rather as one might speak today of a modern American President's 'kitchen cabinet'. Macaulay commented on the word in his *History of England*: 'These ministers were emphatically called the Cabal, and they soon made the appellation so infamous that it has never since ... been used except as a term of reproach.'

PEOPLE, II

The next group consists of words which describe people's opinions or their geographical position.

Tory was an Irish Gaelic word for a pursuer or robber, originally applied to the dispossessed seventeenth-century Irish outlaws who plundered the English settlers; then to the supporters of the Stuart kings against the Hanoverians, and later to those upholding the authority of Church and State. It was in opposition first to Whig, then to Liberal or Radical. (In the US it meant those colonists who continued loyal to George III during the American War of Independence.) It was superseded by Conservative as the name of a British political party.

Johnson defines Tory as 'One who adheres to the antient constitution of the state, and the apostolical hierarchy of the church of England, opposed to a whig.' This makes it pretty clear where he stood, since he defines Whig merely as 'the name of a faction'.

In the days when Toryism meant support for the Stuarts, the two ancient universities, Oxford and Cambridge, were identified with Toryism and Whiggism respectively. When the Hanoverian George I made a present of a library to Cambridge, Joseph Trapp wrote an epigram about that:

> The King, observing with judicious eyes
> The state of both his universities
> To Oxford sent a troop of horse, and why?
> That learned body wanted loyalty;
> To Cambridge books, as very well discerning
> How much that loyal body wanted learning.

To which Sir William Browne replied:

> The King to Oxford sent a troop of horse,
> For Tories own no argument but force:
> With equal skill to Cambridge books he sent,
> For Whigs admit no force but argument.

Now another political word. A **candidate** ought really to be dressed in white. (Tennis or cricket clothes, perhaps?) The word comes from the Latin *candidatus*, 'white-robed'. Candidates for office in ancient Rome wore white togas. Though Shakespeare does not actually use the word, that is what is happening in *Coriolanus*, where the hero appears in 'the gown of humility' to seek election to the consulship. It was loose at the front, so that the aspirant for office could show the scars he had received in battle.

People entered for examination are of course candidates too. They don't wear special clothes, except apparently at Oxford.

rival comes from the Latin *rivalis*, which originally meant someone living on the opposite bank of a river (*rivalis*) from someone else. One can easily see how this would give rise to the modern meaning, since the two people might both want the water or the fish, or might each want to instal a water mill; in any case, since a river is often a boundary, we may imagine hostile landowners glaring at each other across it.

By the sixteenth century, the word had come to mean someone seeking the same object as another person. In *A Midsummer Night's Dream* Helena scolds the two young lovers, Lysander and Demetrius, saying

> You both are rivals, and love Hermia:
> And now both rivals, to mock Helena.

A rival may also be someone who more generally contends with someone else for distinction, which gives rise to 'unrivalled', meaning peerless.

A **cynic** gets the name from a school of ascetic philosophers in ancient Greece, of whom the most famous was Diogenes. He is said to have lived in a tub, and to have taken a lantern by daylight to search for an honest man. His group were named *kunikos*, from *kuōn*, 'dog', perhaps with reference to their way of life. In Milton's masque *Comus* (1634), the tempter refers scornfully to this ascetic tradition:

> O foolishness of men! that lend their ears
> To those budge doctors of the Stoic fur
> And fetch their precepts from the Cynic tub,
> Praising the lean and sallow Abstinence!

Out of this sense grows the meaning of 'cynical' as we understand it today: disbelieving in human sincerity and goodness.

A **barbarian** is, by origin, simply someone foreign or outlandish, and the main thing that struck the first users of the word was that foreigners 'talk funny': the Greek *barbaros* apparently meant something like 'stammering'. The word was first used of people not Greek, and then of people outside the Roman Empire, regarded as wild and uncultured. In reference to Renaissance Italy it meant 'not Italian', which is what Iago probably means in *Othello* when he says that 'a frail vow between an erring barbarian and a supersubtle Venetian' cannot be permanent; though as Othello is not only not Italian but is a black man from North Africa, Iago may mean 'someone from Barbary', the old name for that African coast, which chiefly implied 'not Christian'.

Later, the word was used of any uncultured lout. Matthew Arnold said, 'I have myself called our aristocratic class Barbarians . . . for reading and thinking they have no great turn.'

pagan, in Latin *paganus*, first meant a country dweller, a rustic. The Christian Latin writers such as St Augustine used the same word to mean a heathen, as opposed to a Christian. The suggestion is that the heathen religions lingered on in country places after Christianity had been accepted in the more urban centres of the Roman Empire.

There was some ambiguity as to whether Jews were pagans. In *The Merchant of Venice* the servant Launcelot Gobbo addresses Shylock's daughter Jessica affectionately as 'Most beautiful pagan, most sweet Jew!'

cockney comes from the Middle English *cokeney*, 'cock's egg'. This may have meant an ordinary egg, or perhaps a small misshapen one, once supposed to be laid by the cock; in any case, this meaning goes back to the fourteenth century. By Chaucer's time, a cockney was a mother's darling or milksop, someone effeminately brought up. Lyly used it like that in *Euphues* (1578): 'I brought thee up like a cockney and thou hast handled me like a cock's-comb, I made more of thee than became a father and thou less of me than beseemed a child.'

The word soon came to be contemptuously applied to towns-folk, particularly Londoners and particularly those born within hearing of Bow Bells, in contrast with those tougher souls who lived in the country and were then the large majority. Cockneys were derided both for their ignorance of rural life and for their general debility. Johnson defines the word (1755) with two senses: '(1) A native of London, by way of contempt. So the cockney did to the eels, when she put them i' th' pasty alive. Shakespeare, *King Lear*. (2) Any effeminate, ignorant, low, mean, despicable citizen.'

Writing in *Blackwood's Magazine* (1817) Lockhart, an admirer of the Lake poets and biographer of Sir Walter Scott, scornfully gave the name 'the Cockney school' to Leigh Hunt, Hazlitt, Shelley, and Keats, who were all more or less Londoners.

A **wetback** is an illegal Mexican immigrant in the USA. He (or presumably also she) got wet from swimming the Rio Grande to cross the frontier. In 1972 the *Observer* reported, 'Last year in California alone, border patrols turned back 27,000 wetbacks . . .'

The word has now been used in other watery contexts; recently of Chinese swimmers from the mainland to Hong Kong.

creole probably comes from the Portuguese *crioulo*, 'home-born slave', and thence from *criar*, 'breed', which is related to 'create'. Such a slave would be bred on a South American estate, in contrast to one shipped from Africa. But the word also meant a descendant of Spanish or French settlers in the New World, with or without some mixture of Black ancestry. Louisiana has been called 'the Creole State'.

A newer sense of creole is of a mixed language, combining

usually English, French, or Portuguese with one of the African languages. When mixed languages are used as a lingua franca or second language, they are technically called a pidgin (q.v.) but when they become the mother tongue of a community they are a creole. In 1965 the Catholic journal the *Tablet* reported: 'Haiti, it appears, may soon have its own vernacular, Creole, in the Mass. They already have a Creole missal . . .'

The Greek word for **pygmy** comes from *pugmē*, which means either the fist or the distance from the elbow to the knuckles. Traditionally pygmies were said to be a cubit tall, which is the length of a forearm. Homer and Herodotus referred to these tiny people as living perhaps in India, or perhaps in Ethiopia; but this was later thought to be a fairy tale. Herodotus' story is of a group of young men exploring the Libyan desert:

After travelling for many days over the sand they saw some trees growing on a level spot; they approached and began to pick the fruit which the trees bore, and while they were doing so were attacked by some little men – of less than middle height – who seized them and carried them off . . . They took their captives through a vast tract of marshy country, and beyond it came to a town, all the inhabitants of which were of the same small stature, and all black.

But Dr Johnson described them as 'a nation fabled to be only three spans high, and after long wars to have been destroyed by cranes', and Swift may have been thinking of them when he invented his Lilliputians.

Sceptical writers assumed that the pygmies that the ancients were talking about must really have been chimpanzees or other anthropoid apes. But in the late nineteenth century dwarf races were actually discovered in equatorial Africa, and visited by the explorer Stanley.

The **Gypsy** people first came to England in the early sixteenth century, supposedly from Egypt, so that they were mistakenly called *Egyptians*. An edict of 1514 records, 'It is ordayned agaynste people callynge themselves Egypcyans, that ne such persons be suffred to come within this realme.' They did not, in fact, 'call themselves Egyptians', and they really came originally from India; their language, Romany, contains elements of the many languages of the countries through which they must have passed.

People certainly mixed up Egyptian and Gypsy. When Cleopatra (who really was Egyptian) betrayed Antony at the battle of Actium in Shakespeare's *Antony and Cleopatra* (1607) he cried: 'O this false soul of Egypt! . . . Like a right Gypsie hath at fast and loose Beguil'd me.' And according to one legend, Gypsies were condemned to ceaseless wandering because they refused to shelter the Virgin and baby Jesus on their flight into Egypt.

Today Gypsies prefer to be called travellers, though that word can cover other nomadic peoples not of genuine Gypsy stock. Despite much criticism of their lifestyle (including the idea that they steal children) they have been much romanticized as symbolic of wild freedom; from Masefield's poem 'I must go down to the sea again, to the vagrant gypsy life', to the lady in the folksong who ran away:

> Last night I slept in a goosefeather bed
> With the sheet turned down so bravely, oh.
> But tonight I shall sleep in the cold open field
> Along with the raggle-taggle gypsies, oh.

Anglo-Indian is an ambiguous expression. In older days it meant a British person living in, or retired from, India, and would be so used by anyone writing about those people's tastes and habits: in 1845, for instance, Acton's *Modern Cookery* comments on 'well-seasoned Anglo-Indian palates' as being able to eat more onions and garlic than the rest of us; and in *The Men who Ruled India* (1963) Philip Woodruff speaks of their taste in dress: 'Even in the last days of Anglo-India an observant eye could detect an additional exuberance in the check tweed, a jauntier angle in the slanting pocket, of the cavalry subaltern on leave from India.'

But the term must always have been confusing, because by the early twentieth century 'Anglo-Indian' was the official word for Eurasians in India, people of mixed Indian and European descent. This is rather misleading, because many of those families must have descended on the European side from other than British parents – Portuguese, for instance, as with Michele d'Cruze, the 'Anglo-Indian' hero of Kipling's story 'His Chance in Life', who quells a religious riot in Orissa.

kith and kin usually go together, and are indeed two old Germanic words. But although most of us know that our kin are our relations, it may be less obvious that our kith are strictly speaking not relations, but neighbours, friends, and acquaintances. Some writers have separated this almost inseparable phrase. As the clerihew has it:

> Adam Smith
> Was disowned by all his kith.
> But he was backed through thick and thin
> By all his kin.

Here are four more or less offensive racial epithets, all of rather uncertain origin:

wog is a nasty word for any foreigner – it used to be said 'the wogs begin at Calais' – but especially a non-white one. This twentieth-century word is mysterious. It may come from *golliwog*, the black doll who used to be represented on Robertson's marmalade jars until political correctness removed him. Or it has been ingeniously explained as short for Wily Oriental Gentleman. But there the matter rests. In practice, the word has been chiefly used of Arabs, or of the Arabic language.

wop, a rude twentieth-century word for an Italian, originated in America, and may come from the Italian dialect word *guappo*, 'bold, showy'. In the States it means an immigrant of Italian or southern European stock, but in British xenophobic use it simply means an Italian. As Uncle Matthew comments in Nancy Mitford's *Pursuit of Love* (1945): 'Frogs . . . are slightly better than Huns or Wops, but abroad is unutterably bloody and foreigners are fiends.'

Yankee is a relatively old word, going back to the eighteenth century. It probably comes from the Dutch *Janke*, a diminutive of the name *Jan*, 'John', that was used as a derisive nickname. At the time of the American Civil War a Yankee was a Northerner, and that is the way the word is used in *Gone with the Wind*. To the rest of the world a Yankee is just an American. In Latin America the word has assumed the Spanish form *Yanqui*, as in 'Yanqui imperialism'.

As the British call an American a Yankee, so an American calls a British person a **Limey**. Limeys were first British sailors, or indeed British ships, and in Australia and New Zealand might be recent British immigrants. The word was originally short for *lime*-juicer. It was compulsory in the British navy, from the eighteenth century, to drink lime-juice as a preventative against scurvy, the disease caused by lack of vitamin C during long voyages.

The next three all have something wrong with them mentally:

A **cretin** was dwarfed and mentally retarded from thyroid deficiency, a condition formerly prevalent in the Swiss Alps and other mountain regions. The word, though, is a corruption of 'Christian', and the name was given to these unfortunate people to underline the fact that they were after all humans and not animals; also, perhaps, that being idiots they were incapable of sin.

imbecile comes from the Latin *imbecillus* = *in*, 'without', + *baculum*, 'stick, staff'. So originally an imbecile was someone with no crutch to lean on, and might be someone weak either in body or in mind.

A **lunatic**, though, has been affected by the moon: Latin *luna*. It was believed that such people had recurring periods of insanity depending on the phases of the moon. The word was used in English as early as Langland's *Piers Plowman* (1393). As Shakespeare wrote in *A Midsummer Night's Dream* (1598):

> The lunatic, the lover, and the poet
> Are of imagination all compact.
> One sees more devils than vast hell can hold;
> That is, the madman . . .

Although the word is no longer used technically by psychiatrists, in popular use a lunatic is anyone crazy. When the gifted syndicate of Chaplin, Mary Pickford, Douglas Fairbanks, and D. W. Griffith took charge of United Artists, someone commented: 'The lunatics have taken over the asylum.'

Our last set are not exactly 'people' at all:

robot is a Czech word, from *robota*, 'forced labour'. In 1921 the Czech writer Karel Čapek wrote a science-fiction play 'R.U.R.', which stood for Rossum's Universal Robots. Like Frankenstein, Rossum created artificial men and women to whom he gave the name 'robots', and the word soon entered the English language. It was needed, indeed, with the development of industrial automation, robot astronauts, and robot-controlled planes. But the modern kind of robot, naturally, is very unlike the humanoid ones of science fiction – such as Douglas Adams's lugubrious Marvin in *The Hitch-hiker's Guide to the Galaxy* (1979), who says things like 'Here I am, brain the size of a planet and they ask me to take you down to the bridge. Call that *job satisfaction*?'

spook is the Dutch word for 'ghost', which first reached us through American English and is still somewhat colloquial as an English word. In American slang, a spook is also a spy; and 'spooked' is 'frightened'. Hemingway uses it like that in *To Have and Have Not* (1937): 'He would get to worrying and get so spooked he wouldn't be any use.' But 'spooked up' is 'excited'. Wodehouse picked up that American expression in *Uncle Fred in the Springtime* (1939): 'I saw one of those Western pictures at our local cinema last night, in which a character described himself as being all spooked up with zip and vinegar. That is precisely how I feel. The yeast of spring is fermenting in my veins, and I am ready for anything.'

incubus and **succubus** go together. They were two sorts of demons that descended on sleeping people: incubus from the Latin *in*, succubus from Latin *sub*, 'under', and both from *cubare*, 'lie'. An incubus was supposed in the Middle Ages to lie on top of sleeping women. As Bullfinch has it in *The Age of Chivalry*, 'Merlin was the son of no mortal father, but of an Incubus; one of a class of beings not absolutely wicked, but far from good, who inhabit the regions of the air.' (Their existence was officially recognized in ecclesiastical and civil law.) A succubus was the corresponding female demon who appeared beneath sleeping men and aroused them to sexual intercourse.

In more recent times an incubus came to be just a nightmare, which might happen to anyone; as when Burton in his *Anatomy of Melancholy* (1631) speaks of 'such as are troubled with Incubus, or witch riden, as we call it, if they lie on their backs'. Later it became anything as oppressive as a nightmare. Livingstone in *Zambesi* (1865) refers to 'the great fact that the Americans have rid themselves of the incubus of slavery'.

By the seventeenth century 'succubus' was another word for whore or strumpet, as in Farquhar's *Constant Couple* (1699): 'Here is an old succubus, madam, that has stole two silver spoons, and says she's your nurse.'

CREATURES

We include here only those creatures which are tolerably familiar, at least in zoos. Many of these names, naturally, come from the languages of their original habitat. The mammals first:

orang-utan comes from the Malay *ōrang hūtan*, 'wild man' or 'forest man'. This tree-dwelling ape of Borneo and Sumatra was believed by some early naturalists to be human. The novelist Thomas Love Peacock took up the idea with enthusiasm, and a central character of his novel *Melincourt* (1817) is the orang-utan baronet Sir Oran Haut-ton, who never learns to speak but who drinks wine, plays the flute and French horn, and is elected to Parliament as representative of a 'rotten borough'. He finally rescues the heroine from the vile clutches of the baddy.

The **chimpanzee** gets its name from Kongo, a language of Angola in West Africa, and has been so called since the first one was brought to England in the eighteenth century. It is the most manlike of the apes, and probably the most intelligent; although the Victorian humorist Calverley warned in his 'Ode to Tobacco':

> . . . those who use fusees
> All grow by slow degrees
> Brainless as chimpanzees
> Meagre as lizards.

More recently, Wendy Cope commented succinctly in *Making Cocoa for Kingsley Amis* (1986): 'Rome wasn't built by chimpanzees.'

gorilla comes from the Greek *Gorillai*. A Carthaginian called Hanno, in the fifth or sixth century BC, discovered on his voyages a tribe of particularly hairy Africans, and the Greek account of the matter gives those people their (supposedly) African name, meaning 'hairy man'. Then, when an American missionary found this hairy anthropoid ape in West Africa in 1847, the creature was given the Greek name.

More recently the word has been used, particularly in America, for a hired thug or strong-arm man; the sort of person employed by American racketeers to terrorize their opponents.

zebra comes, through either Italian or Portuguese, from the Congolese name for the animal. The word has existed in English since the sixteenth century, though zebras must have been known in Europe earlier: Gibbon speaks of how 'twenty zebras displayed their elegant forms and variegated beauty to the eyes of the Roman people'.

'Zebra' has naturally been used to mean a number of striped things, such as a striped prison uniform or particularly the British pedestrian crossing with Belisha beacons.

The recently extinct zebra-like **quagga** lived in South Africa and got its name from the Bantu language Xhosa. According to *Nature*, the last surviving quagga died in 1883, in the Amsterdam Zoo.

A creature which only appears to come from West Africa is the **guinea-pig**, which sounds like *Guinea*, the European name of part of the West African coast. But guinea-pigs, curiously, do not originate in Guinea at all, but in South America. This is apparently because in the seventeenth century 'Guinea' was used indiscriminately to mean any mysterious country a long way off.

Later, 'guinea-pig' came also to mean a young midshipman on an Indiaman, on whose behalf substantial fees were paid to the captain. It has been suggested that just as a guinea-pig is neither a pig nor from Guinea, so a midshipman was neither a sailor nor an officer.

The guinea-pig is indeed an anomalous sort of animal. Generations of children have been puzzled by the old saying, 'If you hold a guinea-pig up by the tail, his eyes drop out': a safe enough statement about a little beast with no tail. In the trial scene in *Alice in Wonderland*, Alice was sniffy about the two guinea-pig jurors, who successively cheered and were 'suppressed by the officers of the court . . . "Come, that finishes the guinea-pigs," thought Alice. "Now we shall get on better."'

Another African animal is the **gnu**, whose name comes from the Bushman language of South Africa. The g is silent, as in gnome. That is the point Michael Flanders made in his song (1956): 'I'm a gnu/A gnother gnu.' There isn't much more to be said about this South African antelope, except for Livingstone's comment (1857): 'The presence of the . . . gnu is always a certain indication of water.'

Still on African animals, a **hippopotamus** is a 'river horse': Greek *hippos*, 'horse', + *potamos*, 'river'. The creature was known to the English medieval world; nobody ever seems to have thought it was actually a horse. As one writer has it:

> Ypotame a wonder beest is
> More than an oliphaunt, I wis.

It has captured the imagination of many writers through the centuries, for its size and habits. Hilaire Belloc wrote in the *Bad Child's Book of Beasts* (1896):

> I shoot the Hippopotamus
> With bullets made of platinum,
> Because if I use leaden ones
> His hide is sure to flatten 'em.

And T. S. Eliot wrote a whole poem about the hippopotamus in 1919, comparing his situation to that of the Church:

> The 'potamus can never reach
> The mango on the mango-tree;
> But fruits of pomegranate and peach
> Refresh the Church from over sea . . .

rhinoceros is Greek: *rhinos*, 'nose', + *keras*, 'horn'. The creature was vaguely known of, by hearsay, to the medieval world, so that its name has existed in English since the fourteenth century; travellers' tales of rhinoceroses may have given rise to the legend of the unicorn. They are proverbially unwieldy and bad-tempered – the latter, according to Kipling's story 'How the Rhinoceros Got His Skin', because their wrinkled skins are full of itchy cake crumbs. But perhaps their most striking appearance in literature is in Eugène Ionesco's French play *Rhinoceros* (1959), an allegory of the Nazi phenomenon. The hero nervously remains human while all his fellow-citizens turn into rhinoceroses and go trampling and trumpeting about in happy conformity.

Powdered rhinoceros horn has been valued for centuries as a potent aphrodisiac.

buffalo comes through Portuguese and Latin, from the Greek word *boubalos*, which meant either an antelope or a wild ox. Today it correctly means one kind of African ox, or another Asian one, the black Indian water buffalo with great horns. But by confusion the same name has been given since the seventeenth century to the North American bison, quite a different creature, which used to roam the prairies in enormous herds; as in *Home on the Range* (1873):

> Oh give me a home where the buffalo roam
> Where the deer and the antelope play . . .

The American kind has somehow had a more voluminous press than the others, what with the exploits of the great hunter Buffalo Bill (William Cody) and his like.

An **armadillo** is a 'little warrior'. This Spanish word is the diminutive of *armado*, 'armed man'. A suitable name, owing to its bony armour. The travel writer John Frampton described it in 1577 in his book *Ioyfull Newes out of the Newe Founde Worlde*: 'He is called the Armadillo, that is to saie a beaste armed.' (It is not clear whether the news of armadillos was particularly ioyfull.)

Its habit of rolling itself into a ball, like a hedgehog, when alarmed, gave Kipling the idea he uses in one of his *Just So Stories* for children (1902) by which the armadillo is a combination of a hedgehog and a tortoise, being able both to roll itself up and to swim.

We move to Australia, where **kangaroo** and **dingo** are both

Aboriginal names for the creatures. Captain Cook in his *Journal* (1770) speaks of 'the animals which I have before mentioned, called by the Natives Kangooroo or Kangaru'. (It is sad to have to repudiate the good legend that an early visitor, seeing the creature lolloping about and asking an Aboriginal its name, was told 'Kanga-roo', meaning 'I don't understand.')

The Kangaroos are an Australian Rugby League team; and an Australian motor vehicle may be fitted with a 'kangaroo bar' in front, to protect the vehicle if it strikes the creature. Outside Australia, a kangaroo closure is the procedure for ending a British parliamentary debate by a committee chairperson who selects the amendments to be discussed, and a kangaroo court of justice is an unofficial one, without legal standing.

The Aboriginal word **dingo** is recorded as early as 1789. These dogs must have been thought badly of in Australia, since dingo is a slang word there for a coward or shirker, and to dingo on someone is to let them down or rat on them.

Both kangaroos and dingoes are immortalized in Kipling's *Just So Stories* (1902), where he recounts how Old Man Kangaroo grew his long legs by being chased by Yellow-Dog Dingo right across Australia.

With **skunk** we move to North America, because this is the animal's North American Indian name, used in that form by the early fur trappers. The appalling smell that it squirts out to discourage its attackers has given it such a bad reputation that its name has long been used for a thoroughly nasty contemptible person, or indeed for anything smelly. In 1973, for instance, the Toronto *Globe & Mail* described how 'thousands of blue-jeaned teenagers . . . drink beer in the sun, drinking it fast so it doesn't go skunky'.

In American military slang, a skunk is an unidentified and per-haps hostile ship.

The North American **racoon**, or raccoon, gets its name from an Algonquian dialect of Virginia. Dr Johnson defined it rather charmingly, and accurately enough: 'The *rackoon* is a New England animal, like a badger, having a tail like a fox, being cloathed with a thick and deep furr: it sleeps in the day time in a hollow tree, and goes out a-nights, when the moon shines, to feed on the sea side, where it is hunted by dogs.' The hunting was for its rich greyish-brown fur, to make 'coonskin' coats, or caps with the creature's striped bushy tail hanging down the back as worn by the likes of Daniel Boone.

We return to Europe for the remaining mammals. The **lemming**, being an arctic creature, gets its name from Norwegian, with related names in Lapp and Swedish. Many legends seem to have attached themselves to these small rodents: early naturalists believed that they fall down from the clouds like rain. It is certainly true that they periodically emigrate, in enormous numbers, from the high mountain chain of Scandinavia downhill towards the sea. The emigration takes up to three years, and they swim any rivers or lakes that lie in the way; the survivors then try to swim the Baltic or the North Sea in the same way, and drown.

This apparent mass suicide of the lemmings has given rise to a sort of modern moralizing rather like that of the medieval bestiaries, which derived lessons on human behaviour from that of animals. People are like lemmings if they rush headlong towards disaster. Perhaps James Thurber had better have the last word on this subject (1942):

'I don't understand,' said the scientist, 'why you lemmings all rush down to the sea and drown yourselves.'

'How curious,' said the lemming. 'The one thing I don't understand is why you human beings don't.'

The **sable** gets its name through Old French from Slavonic; understandably, since this small quadruped lives mostly in sub-arctic Siberia. Its beautiful fur has been known since at least the fifteenth century. In the reign of Henry VIII it was ordained 'that none under the degree of an earl shall use sables'.

It is a puzzle that 'sable' is also the word for black in heraldry, although the animal is in fact dark brown. (Some have suggested that sable fur may often have been dyed black to contrast better with ermine, since the two furs would often be combined in ceremonial robes.)

Sable came to be a poetic word for black, or for black mourning clothes. The Lady in Milton's *Comus* (1634) wonders:

> Was I deceived, or did a sable cloud
> Turn forth her silver lining on the night?

At a crisis in the affairs of the paynim knight Sir Palomides in T. H. White's *Once and Future King* (1958), the Highland women exclaim sympathetically, 'Ah, the puir churl! The sassenagh! The sable savage! Will he no' come back again?' And at Amelia's mother's funeral in Thackeray's *Vanity Fair* (1848), 'Her little boy sat by her side in pompous new sables.'

The **ermine** is probably an *Armenian* (mouse). It is in fact a stoat, but in cold countries its fur turns white by moulting, except for the black tip of the tail. It is this combination of white fur decorated with black tail tips that has been the traditional trimming of stately robes from early times.

The ancient kingdom of Armenia included the Caucasus, so there may well have been white ermines up there in the winter.

spaniel comes from the Old French word *espaigneul*, 'Spanish'. The Irish were the first users of spaniels, as hunting dogs, and probably got them originally from Spain. Spaniels are mentioned in the Irish laws of AD 17. They were used in the Middle Ages as retrievers in falconry, and occur in Chaucer. Charles II gave his name to the miniature King Charles spaniel, his favourite breed.

But the chief 'folklore', so to speak, about spaniels is that they are servile and fawn on people. Shakespeare's Henry VIII reproves the Bishop of Winchester for flattery, saying

> To me you cannot reach you play the spaniel
> And think with wagging of your tongue to win me.

Dr Johnson makes no bones about it in his *Dictionary*. One of his senses of spaniel is 'A low, mean, sneaking fellow; a courtier; a dedicator; a pensioner; a dependant; a placeman.'

The **poodle** must have started life as a German water-dog: the German *pudelhund* is related to the German word for 'puddle'. The name does not seem to have occurred in English until the 1820s, but there is a poodle in Goethe's *Faust* (1808): it is the form in which the tempter Mephistopheles first appears to Faust.

As poodles are usually pet dogs, the word has often been used for a servile lackey or cat's-paw. In 1907 Lloyd George accused the House of Lords of being 'Mr Balfour's Poodle'.

mammoth is a Russian word, *mamo(n)t*. That is what the creature was called by the ivory hunters of Siberia. The enormous tusks of frozen mammoths were exported from there to China and Europe from medieval times, so that the word was known in English from about 1700. As an adjective, mammoth came to mean 'enormous'. When a very large cheese was presented to Thomas Jefferson during his presidency, wags called it the Mammoth Cheese. More recently the *Economist* (1974) referred to our 'mammoth current account deficit'.

A **porcupine** is a 'prickly pig': from the Latin *porcus*, 'pig', + *spina*, 'thorn'. Since the creature exists in south-eastern Europe it was known to the medieval world. They believed that it could shoot its quills at an enemy, which made James I of Scotland write in 1423 of 'the werely [i.e. warlike] porcupine'. Louis XIV of France went so far in 1394 as to create an Order of the Porcupine.

Shakespeare called it a porpentine, as he does where the Ghost tells Hamlet that the horrors of Purgatory would make

> each particular hair to stand on end,
> Like quills upon the fretful porpentine.

Sir Thomas Browne noted in his *Vulgar Errors* (1646) that it copulates 'pronely, that is by contaction of the prone parts in both', presumably on account of the prickles; and Dr Johnson commented in his *Dictionary* that it has 'ears very like those of the human species'. Hilaire Belloc gives some sensible advice, in *More Beasts for Worse Children*, against slapping it:

> To strike the meanest and the least
> Of creatures is a sin,
> How much more bad to beat a beast
> With prickles on its skin.

cattle has been with us, of course, for many centuries. The interesting thing is that the Old French word *chatel*, which it comes from, means 'chattel', which goes back to the Latin for 'capital', one's wealth or property. This came to mean one's livestock, the most obvious form of personal possession. At first it included all one's camels, horses, sheep, pigs, and so on, even one's hens and bees. (The 'cattle shed' where baby Jesus was born traditionally housed an ass as well as an ox.)

By the sixteenth century cattle chiefly meant cows, or sometimes horses, and in *Uncle Tom's Cabin* (1850) Harriet Beecher Stowe records its use to mean slaves: 'What have any of you cussed cattle to do with thinking what's right?'

Next, some birds:

albatross comes from *alcatraz* in Spanish and Portuguese, and ultimately from an Arabic word *alḳādūs*, 'bucket'. All this for the strange reason that *alcatraz* first meant the pelican, whose great beak looks like one of the buckets of a water-raising wheel for irrigation. The name was then vaguely applied to other sea birds, such as the gannet and the frigate bird. (The prison island Alcatraz near San Francisco was once crowded with sea birds.) The word settled down some time in the eighteenth century with the spelling 'albatross', to mean the great Pacific and southern ocean bird that it means today. Sailors say it is fatal to shoot an albatross, which accounts for the curse that descended on Coleridge's Ancient Mariner (1798), when he shot one with his crossbow. (In fact, the bird is much too big to be hung round anyone's neck, as they did with him in the poem.)

Because of Coleridge, the word has since been used to mean a handicap or encumbrance. In 1994, for instance, the *Economist* remarked that 'Perpetually visible waste, in need of constant protection and monitoring, is an albatross around the neck of the [nuclear] industry.' But the British golfing sense, in which an albatross is the rare score of three strokes under par, takes the name of an albatross as an even bigger bird to mean something even cleverer than a 'birdie' (one stroke under) or an 'eagle' (two under).

cockatoo comes from the Malay *kakatua*. The name of this Australian and East Indian crested parrot perhaps imitates the noise it makes, as with the cuckoo. Cockatoos must have been brought back to England by sailors quite early – they are mentioned in 1616 by the playwrights Beaumont and Fletcher – and have been traditionally kept as cage-birds; though as Shaw acidly commented in *Getting Married* (1911): 'Home life as we understand is no more natural to us than a cage is natural to a cockatoo.'

In Australia and New Zealand, a cockatoo is a small arable farmer, so called rather scornfully by the prosperous and influential squatters. In 1874 a visitor to those parts recorded: 'Like a cockatoo, the small freeholder alights on good ground, extracts all he can from it, and then flies away.'

The **budgerigar** is also an Australian parrot, and its name is Australian: the Aboriginal word may or may not be built up from *budgeri*, 'good', and *gar*, 'cockatoo'. It is not clear what is specially 'good' about them. They seem to have become popular as cage-birds only late in the last century, perhaps as part of a general modern tendency for things kept in cages to get smaller; hamsters and jerboas rather than guinea-pigs.

bantam is named, apparently by mistake, from *Bañtān* in the north-west of Java. These fowls may have been imported into Europe from Java, but they are originally Japanese. The cocks are aggressive fighters, which gave the name to various 'bantam divisions' and 'bantam battalions' of undersized soldiers in the First World War. In boxing, wrestling and weightlifting, 'bantam-weight' is heavier than flyweight but lighter than featherweight: another association with fighting.

The **turkey** does not come from Turkey at all, but from North America. Its name was first given to the African guinea-fowl, which was indeed imported into Europe through Turkey, and later applied to the familiar Christmas dinner bird, which was found to be already domesticated in sixteenth-century Mexico. The French call it *dindon*, or *dinde*, 'from India', which is wrong too.

In the sixteenth century, when turkeys were a novelty, the

saying arose, 'Turkeys, heresy, hops, and beer/ Came into England all in one year.'

This bird has given rise to some lively idioms: to talk turkey is to get down to business; cold turkey is the treatment of drug addicts by the abrupt withdrawal of the drug; and in the American theatre a turkey is a theatrical flop.

The **dodo** was a 'simpleton', from the Portuguese *doudo*. This large, clumsy, flightless bird lived on the islands of Mauritius and Reunion until it was exterminated by man and by the other creatures, such as hogs, which he imported to the islands. The Portuguese name suggests that it was too stupid to survive.

It is not clear whether dodos were good to eat. Oliver Goldsmith wrote in his *Natural History* (1774): 'Three or four dodos are enough to dine a hundred men.' But he can never have eaten one, as they no longer existed by then; and the Dutch called them *walgvogels*, 'disgusting birds', since they were so unpalatable. They seem to have been chiefly noticed in our language and literature for being extinct. The title story of Angus Wilson's *Such Darling Dodos* (1950) is about an elderly couple who had failed to move with the times.

And now reptiles:

crocodile is Greek: *krokē*, 'pebble', + *drilos*, 'worm'. The creature has been so called since at least the time of Herodotus, since the ancients knew the crocodiles of the Nile. Crocodiles have attracted many curious beliefs throughout the ages. In the first century A D Plutarch wrote, 'The Egyptians worship God symbolically in the crocodile, that being the only animal without a tongue, like the Divine Logos, which standeth not in need of speech.' Crocodiles were thought, as Lepidus remarks during a drunken orgy in *Antony and Cleopatra*, to be 'bred out of your mud by the operation of your sun'. This theory of spontaneous generation arose because, as Johnson explains at some length in his *Dictionary*: '*Crocodiles* lay their eggs . . . on the sand near the waterside, covering them with the sand, that the heat of the sun may contribute to hatch them.'

Johnson did not believe, as many earlier writers did, that the crocodile shed hypocritical tears to attract its human prey – 'in false grief hiding his harmful guile', as Spenser put it in *The Faerie Queene* (1590) – but he did think that it had scented dung. As a twelfth-century bestiary puts it, 'Its dung provides an ointment with which old and wrinkled whores anoint their figures and are made beautiful, until the flowing sweat of their efforts washes it away.'

The word 'crocodile' for a procession of schoolchildren walking in pairs has been used in Britain since Victorian times.

The **alligator** is a New World member of the crocodile family. Accordingly, its name is Spanish: *el lagarto*, 'the lizard'. The Spanish for 'the', in fact, has become part of the name – Ralegh called the creature 'lagartos'. The word was known in English under various spellings by the sixteenth century: in *Romeo and Juliet*, Romeo visits an apothecary to buy some poison, and notices that

> . . . in his needy shop a tortoise hung,
> An alligator stuff'd, and other skins
> of ill-shaped fishes . . .

There seems to be no particular reason, other than rhyme, for the fifties song 'See you later, alligator.'

The **newt** and the **adder** come in here only because something odd has happened to the beginnings of these medieval words. 'An ewt' became 'a newt', and conversely 'a nadder' became 'an adder'. It seems that the n of 'an' is apt to slide to and fro. The shift had happened by the fifteenth century, so that the witches in *Macbeth* naturally cooked 'eye of newt and toe of frog' in their cauldron.

In modern literature, newts feature chiefly as the beloved pets of Wodehouse's Gussie Fink-Nottle: 'Do you know how a male newt proposes, Bertie? He just stands in front of the female newt vibrating his tail and bending his body in a semi-circle. I could do that on my head.'

dinosaur comes from the Greek *deinos*, 'terrible', and *sauros*, 'lizard'. Perhaps it is because they really did once exist that dinosaurs have become so popular today in the folk imagination, as witnessed by the recent success of the film *Jurassic Park*. They seem to have superseded dragons, which are unfortunately mythical. And because they are both enormous and extinct, the word has come to be used of any large unwieldy organization that is out of date.

The modern French for **crayfish** or **crawfish** is *écrevisse*, which goes back to similar words in medieval and older French. But as the creature lives in the water, English speakers naturally assumed that the last syllable was 'fish'. From its habit of getting out of holes backwards, the Americans have made a useful verb that means to retreat from a position, literally or figuratively: one crawfishes out of an embarrassing situation.

The **tarantula** spider gets its name from the seaport *Taranto* in the heel of Italy, and so does the rapid whirling dance called the **tarantella**, but the connection between the two is not clear. There was indeed a sort of hysterical dancing mania, called 'tarantism', particularly prevalent in those parts from the fifteenth to the seventeenth century, and some believed that the dancing was caused by the bite of the spider. On the other hand, it was also believed that music and dancing cured the bite. Johnson defined the creature in his *Dictionary* as 'an insect whose bite is only cured by musick'; and Samuel Pepys was told in 1662 about the tarantula, that 'all the harvest long (about which time they are most busy) there are fiddlers go up and down the fields everywhere, in expectation of being hired by those that are stung'.

Perhaps the dance imitates the antics of the people who are bitten. Many distinguished musicians such as Liszt and Chopin have written tarantellas: very fast pieces in six-eight time.

PLANTS

First come some edible fruits and vegetables:

banana comes, through either Portuguese or Spanish, from the local name of this tropical fruit in West Africa. Its existence was reported in English by travellers as early as the seventeenth century; though we can scarcely have eaten bananas here until comparatively recent times, when they started to reach us on 'banana boats'. 'Banana republic' is a rude way of referring to the small states of Central America whose economy depends on exporting fruit. And one should not forget the slippery 'banana skin' underfoot that traditionally trips up the unwary. In 1961 Trevor-Roper wrote of 'the love of . . . laying banana-skins to disconcert the gravity and upset the balance of the orthodox'.

The **potato** is commonly supposed to have been introduced into Ireland, and thence into England, by Sir Walter Ralegh in about 1584; but the matter is confused by nobody's being quite sure whether early references to the plant mean the potato as we know it or the 'sweet potato'. The name comes through Spanish from *batata*, its native name in Haiti in the American Indian language Taino. Potatoes were becoming a common food in England, and particularly in Ireland, by the late seventeenth century – to the dismay of some people such as the Radical agitator William Cobbett. In his *Cottage Economy* (1821) he referred to the potato as 'the lazy root . . . the root also of slovenliness, filth, misery, and slavery; its cultivation has increased in England with the increase of the paupers'. Certainly the tragic results of depending entirely on the potato were shown in the Irish Potato Famine of 1846–7, when the crop failed.

A 'hot potato' of course is something one must drop quickly. In 1963 the *Listener* reported, 'Tories continue to treat *laissez-faire* enterprise as a political hot potato.' And a 'couch potato' is someone who does nothing all day but sit and watch television.

The **tomato** came originally, like the potato, from the New World. Its name reached us through French or Spanish or Portuguese from *tomatl* in Nahuatl, a language of Mexico. It was seen growing in its native tropical America in the early seventeenth century, and was later naturalized here; though as gardeners know, it does not flourish in our climate as readily as the potato. Since one of the obvious things about this fruit is its bright colour, 'tomato' has come to be used for a particular shade of red, chiefly by fashion writers.

The common American pronunciation of the word, to rhyme with potato, gave rise to Gershwin's song in 1937:

> You like potato and I like po-tah-to,
> You like tomato and I like to-mah-to . . .

avocado is Spanish for 'advocate'. This name was apparently substituted (because easier to say) for the original Aztec *ahuacatl*, 'testicle' (presumably describing the shape). The fruit was first mentioned by voyagers in the seventeenth century, but as with the banana we cannot grow it here.

The **Jerusalem artichoke** gets the Jerusalem part of its name from the Italian *girasole*, 'sunflower'. The name means that sunflowers 'turn' to the 'sun'. This plant is indeed a kind of sunflower; its edible tubers are thought to taste like the real or 'globe' artichoke, a kind of thistle. (The artichoke part, by the way, is Arabic: *al-karšūfa*.)

As so often, this name has been Anglicized to make it easier to say. As the Reverend Doctor Opimian explains in Thomas Love Peacock's *Gryll Grange* (1860), the plant is 'a girasol, or turn-to-the-sun. From this girasol we have made Jerusalem, and from the Jerusalem artichoke we make Palestine soup.'

The **apricot** gets its name, by a tortuous route through Portuguese or Spanish, Arabic, and Greek from the Latin *praecox*, 'early ripe', as in 'precocious'. (They do indeed flower as early as February, which makes it difficult to protect the flowers from frost in our climate.) The fruit has been known here at least since Shakespeare's day: in *King Richard II* the head gardener instructs a subordinate,

> Go, bind thou up yon dangling apricocks,
> Which, like unruly children, make their sire
> Stoop with oppression of their prodigal weight.

More recently, in Surtees's *Handley Cross* (1843), we are advised to clean boot tops with champagne and apricot jam.

The **currant**, being grown around the eastern Mediterranean, was first called a raisin of *Corinth*. The English seem to have been eating these small seedless dried grapes since the fourteenth century, as they are mentioned in medieval cookery books. Currants are on the shopping list which Perdita in *The Winter's Tale* gave her foster-brother: 'Three pound of sugar; five pound of currants; rice . . .'

Then, some time in the sixteenth century, blackcurrants and redcurrants were introduced into English gardens, and were at first believed to be the source of the more familiar sort of currant. Dr Johnson liked them. When he was advising Boswell on what to grow in his Scottish garden, he commented, 'I would plant a great many currants; the fruit is good, and they make a pretty sweetmeat.' And readers of Louisa Alcott's *Good Wives* (1869) may remember the young housewife Meg's disastrous attempt to make currant jelly.

The **greengage** was introduced into England in the eighteenth century, from France, by the botanist Sir William Gage, and in England it takes his name. In France, though, this plum is called a *reine-Claude*, after one of their sixteenth-century queens.

In rhyming slang the greengage is the stage, and greengages are wages.

The **damson** is supposedly a plum of *Damascus*. Damsons were indeed introduced into Greece and Italy from Syria, in the Middle Ages.

peach comes from the Latin *persicum*, 'Persian (plum)'. The tree was certainly brought into Europe from Asia, but in quite early times, and the word has existed in English since the fourteenth century. Chaucer mentions it in the *Romance of the Rose* (?1366), and the poet Andrew Marvell was eating peaches in the seventeenth century:

> The nectarine and curious peach
> Into my hands themselves do reach.

Eliot's 'J. Alfred Prufrock' noticed in 1917 that peaches are messy:

> I grow old . . . I grow old . . .
> I shall wear the bottoms of my trousers rolled.
> Shall I part my hair behind? Do I dare to eat a peach?

Peaches have nothing to do with the verb to peach, 'turn informer, split on someone'. That is related to 'impeach'.

rhubarb comes from two Greek words, *rha* (probably an ancient name for the river Volga), + *barbaros*, 'foreign'. There are effectively two sorts of rhubarb; the familiar garden one with edible pinkish stalks, and a Chinese and Tibetan one of the same genus whose root has been used as a purgative in medicine from very early times; in China, indeed, since 2700 BC. The Chinese drug reached Europe by the fifteenth century, travelling by a long route through Persia to Aleppo and Syria. That is the kind Macbeth is talking about when he expostulates to Lady Macbeth's doctor:

> What rhubarb, senna, or what purgative drug
> Would scour these English hence?

English garden rhubarb has been grown here since the seventeenth century, though that too is of Asiatic origin.

'Rhubarb, rhubarb' is traditionally what a crowd of actors say to give an impression of murmuring hubbub. Consequently the word can mean nonsense, rubbish. In 1977 the *Times Literary Supplement* censured an opera company as having 'a huge repertoire consisting almost entirely of rhubarb'.

tapioca, that infamous ingredient of old-fashioned school milk puddings, comes from *tipioca* in Tupi, a language of the Amazon. It is produced from the roots of the cassava plant, and its Tupi name consists of *tipi*, 'dregs', + *og* or *ok*, 'squeeze out'.

Tapioca has been with us for centuries without anyone's ever seeming to like it very much. In Kipling's *Life's Handicap* (1891) he describes four men, on an intolerably hot night somewhere in the middle of India, sitting down to a nasty dinner of 'the miserable goat-chops, and the smoked tapioca pudding'.

The plant **arrowroot** gets its English name because the tubers were used in the West Indies to absorb poison from the wounds of poisoned arrows. As was recorded in 1788, 'It is esteemed a sovereign remedy against the bite of wasps, and the poison of the manchineel tree.' Arrowroot makes a bland, starchy pudding that used to be given to invalids.

It is sometimes hard to imagine what Europeans ate before they discovered America! But when we move from tapioca and arrowroot to **sago**, another sort of milk pudding, we come to the Malay word *sāgū*, which reached us through Portuguese. Hakluyt mentions it in his account of Sir Francis Drake's voyages, about 1580: 'We receiued of them meale, which they call Sagu . . . made of the tops of certaine trees . . . whereof they make certaine cakes.' It is in fact the starchy pith of the sago palm.

cereals come from the Latin *cerealis*, which refers to *Ceres*. She was the Roman goddess of agriculture and the fruits of the earth. Besides meaning wheat, oats, rice, etc., the word now often means breakfast foods such as cornflakes. (Which, incidentally, are made of maize, because that is what 'corn' means in America.)

And **maize** comes to us through Spanish; originally from the name of this cereal plant in Carib, a language of the southern West Indies. Just as the British need to grasp that cornflakes are made of maize, and that maize is in question in Oscar Hammerstein's song about 'The corn is as high as an elephant's eye', so the Americans may not understand that the Corn Laws repealed by Sir Robert Peel were about wheat, and that when Ruth 'stood in tears amid the alien corn' in Keats's 'Ode to a Nightingale', wheat was what she was standing amid.

spinach comes through various languages, but ultimately from the Persian *ispānāk*. The name may be connected with the Latin for 'spine', because of its prickly seeds. English speakers seem to have been eating the stuff since the sixteenth century. On Easter Sunday, 1773, Boswell with mingled excitement and trepidation dined with Johnson: 'I supposed we should scarcely have knives and forks, and only some strange, uncouth, ill-dressed fish: but . . . we had a very good soup, a boiled leg of lamb and spinach, a veal pye, and a rice pudding.'

Spinach has traditionally been thought to be particularly good for you. The celebrated cartoon character 'Popeye the Sailorman', when on the point of being beaten up by the baddy, would swallow a tin of spinach and become suddenly invincible. 'Gammon and spinach' or just 'gammon' alone, means nonsense. The combined phrase first appeared as the refrain of the old song 'A frog he would a-wooing go':

> With a rowley, powley, gammon and spinach,
> Heigho, says Anthony Rowley!

Dickens knew the expression. In *David Copperfield* (1850) he has Miss Mowcher remark to Steerforth and Copperfield, 'What a world of gammon and spinnage it is, though, ain't it?' when she feels surrounded by a lot of pretentious humbug. And in colloquial American use, 'spinach' alone means the same thing.

nutmeg comes through Old French from the Latin *nux*, 'nut', + *muscus*, 'musk'. This aromatic spice from the East Indian 'spice islands' apparently reached us by the Middle Ages. Chaucer in his 'Tale of Sir Thopas' (*c.* 1386) mentions 'notemuge to put in ale'. Nutmegs came from the Moluccas, and the Dutch tried to control their export, but were frustrated by a particular kind of pigeon which fed on the fruit and then flew away. It was believed in nineteenth-century America that the inhabitants of Connecticut fraudulently manufactured and sold wooden nutmegs, which gave Connecticut the name of the Nutmeg State.

saffron is an Arabic word: *za'farān*. This yellow food flavouring and colouring is made of the dried stigmas of crocuses, and was already popular in Britain in the Middle Ages. The cookery writer Elizabeth David suggests that the use of saffron was first introduced to the West by the Phoenicians, for bouillabaisse and other Provençal food. It is very expensive to produce, as it takes about 170,000 flowers to make a kilo of saffron. There must have once been great fields of crocuses at the Essex town which is still called Saffron Walden.

And now a few flowers:

A **dandelion** is a 'lion's tooth': *dent-de-lion* in French; apparently from the toothy shape of the leaves. It scarcely belongs with edible plants, except that one can make a sort of coffee with the powdered roots, and feed the leaves to one's rabbits.

The reason why the **dahlia**, the **fuchsia**, and particularly the **eschscholtzia** furnish such popular material for spelling-bees is that these flowers all commemorate the names of foreign botanists. The dahlia was introduced into Europe from Mexico in 1789, and named in honour of the Swedish botanist *Dahl* who died in that year. The fuchsia commemorates a sixteenth-century German botanist, Leonard *Fuchs*. And the yellow poppy eschscholtzia is called after another German botanist, of the early nineteenth century, J. F. von *Eschscholtz*, who discovered it when exploring in California.

Next come some trees:

teak comes from *tekka* in Malayalam, a language of south India. This tropical tree grows in monsoon forests. Its hard, heavy wood was important in earlier days for shipbuilding, and later for railway carriages.

bamboo, not really a tree but a sort of enormous grass, gets its name from Malay. The word existed in English as early as the sixteenth century, and is both noun and verb. (To 'bamboo' someone was, of course, to beat them with a bamboo.) Bamboo is also a colour: in the eighteenth century Josiah Wedgwood invented a cane-coloured porcelain, which he called 'bamboo'.

The 'bamboo curtain', an expression coined on the pattern of

47

'iron curtain', is the barrier between the territories controlled by Communist China and the adjacent non-communist countries.

raffia comes from Malagasy, the language of Madagascar. That is where the palm tree *raphia* first grew. The raffia we know is the fibre from its leaves, mostly used for tying up things in gardens; though let us not forget the Mrs Joyful Prize for Raffia Work, as awarded at St Custard's in Willans and Searles's *Down with Skool*.

The **sequoia** is called after *Sequoia*, a nineteenth-century Chero-kee Indian scholar of the southern United States. He invented a syllabary alphabet for writing the Cherokee language. Strictly speaking, the name belongs to either of two huge Californian conifers, which can both live for over 2000 years and grow to over 300 feet tall. One of them, the Giant Sequoia, may be better known in British parks and gardens as the **wellingtonia**, the name given to it here in the nineteenth century by the English botanist Lindley. He called it after the great Duke of Wellington. As the *Gardener's Chronicle* explained in 1853: 'Wellington stands as high above his contemporaries as the Californian tree above all the surrounding foresters. Let it then bear henceforward the name of *Wellingtonia gigantea.*'

mahogany is a mystery. Nobody seems to know where this seventeenth-century word came from. It means any of various tropical trees originating in Indonesia, Australia, or the rain forests of Central America. Since the reddish-brown wood is much used for furniture, the word came to mean a dining-table. In Dickens's *Old Curiosity Shop* (1840) the deplorable Sampson Brass, when cornered, remarks, 'I had hoped to see you three gentlemen, one day or another, with your legs under the mahogany in my humble parlour in the Marks.'

Mahogany also means a reddish-brown colour, particularly of human skin. In Thackeray's *Vanity Fair* (1848) George Osborne is nasty about the court dress of Rhoda Swartz, the good-natured heiress from the West Indies whom his father wants him to marry: 'Diamonds and mahogany, my dear! think what an advantageous contrast . . .'

THE BODY,
AND ITS EMBELLISHMENTS
AND PROBLEMS

muscle comes from the Latin *musculus*, 'little mouse'. Apparently the Romans thought that some muscles, such as the biceps, wriggled like mice: 'The muscles of his brawny arms/ Are strong as iron bands,' as Longfellow wrote in 1839. This has been an English word since the sixteenth century, and the Victorians used the phrase 'muscular Christianity' for the Christian life of strenuous physical activity advocated by Charles Kingsley, vigorous author of *Westward Ho!* and *The Water Babies*.

The **goolies**, or testicles, come from the Hindi *golí*, 'ball, bullet', and originally from Sanskrit. This word has probably been with us since the last century, but passed into the written language only in these more permissive times. Sue Townsend's hero in *The Secret Diary of Adrian Mole* (1982) can now recount: 'Woke up with a pain in my goolies. Told my mother. She wanted to look but I didn't want her to so she said I would have to soldier on.'

Curiously, an Australian slang use has reverted more closely to the Sanskrit original. In Australia a goolie is a pebble.

The **duodenum**, the first part of the small intestine, is so called from its length. It is supposed to be as long as the breadth of twelve fingers; hence the Latin name *duodenum* (= twelve) *digitorum* (= fingers' breadths). The term has been used in anatomy since the fourteenth century.

The most attractive, though not universally accepted, explanation of **funny-bone** is that it is a rather ponderous pun on the Latin *humerus*, the technical term for the upper bone of the arm. The trouble is that though a knock on one's funny-bone gives one a strange feeling, there is nothing funny about it in the 'humorous' sense. There the matter rests.

When you use your **loaf**, you are using a bit of abbreviated rhyming slang: *loaf* of bread = head. Your loaf in this sense is of course your common sense, or gumption.

tattoo is no less than three words, of wildly different origins. The one that means a design pricked into the skin is Polynesian, recorded by Captain Cook in 1769: 'This method of Tattowing I shall now describe . . . As this is a painful operation, especially the Tattowing their Buttocks, it is performed but once in their Life times.'

The military tattoo, though, the evening signal for soldiers to go to bed, is of Dutch origin: *taptoe*, 'close the tap (of the cask)'. In 1644 a military order decreed, 'If anyone shall bee found tiplinge or drinkinge in any Taverne, Inne, or Alehouse after the houre of nyne of the clock at night, when the Tap-too beates, hee shal pay 2s 6d.' This word also means an evening military entertainment, like the one at Edinburgh Castle during the Festival, with music and marching and perhaps a sword dance.

A third kind of tattoo is a sort of pony bred in India: Hindi *ṭaṭṭū*. The poet Robert Southey observed in 1814 that 'A Mahratta wife . . . frequently rides astride . . . upon a bullock, an ass, or a little tattoo horse.'

Now come some things that can go wrong with the body.

Several of these words have the odd characteristic of being the plural of an older singular word. For instance, **measles** is the plural of the early Dutch *masel*, 'a spot or blister'. It was formerly confused with the old word *mesel*, 'leprosy', so that in early writing it is sometimes not clear which of these two very different diseases is meant. (*Mesel* is the Latin *misellus*, 'wretched'.) In Malory's *Morte D'Arthur* (1469) there is a poor lady who 'Whanne she had layne a grete whyle she felle vnto a mesel.'

Measles seldom strikes twice, and is perhaps best got over early in life. As Jerome K. Jerome (of *Three Men in a Boat*) wrote: 'Love is like the measles; we all have to go through it.' And Albert

Einstein struck a more serious note: 'Nationalism is an infantile sickness. It is the measles of the human race.'

Another hidden plural lurks in **pox**, and consequently in **small-pox**. The singular word is *pock*, 'pustule', from Old English; one may still recognize the expression 'pock-marked'. As one always has more than one pustule, various diseases came to be called *pocks*, and then to be spelt 'pox'. ('Pock' need not always mean a disease. Sherlock Holmes adorned his wall with 'a patriotic V.R. done in bullet-pocks'.)

Smallpox is now, happily, eradicated. It was so called to distinguish it from the 'great pox', or 'French pox' or 'Spanish pox', which all meant syphilis. Byron commented in *Don Juan* (1819):

> I said the small-pox has gone out of late;
> Perhaps it may be followed by the great.

But 'pox' on its own has chiefly meant syphilis for a long time; as in Pope's third *Moral Essay* (1731), in which the over-ambitious citizen's daughter 'flaunts a Viscount's tawdry wife;/ She bears a Coronet and P-x for life'.

mumps is the plural of *mump*, which meant a 'grimace'; understandably, as that is how people look who have got the disease.

The vitamin D deficiency disease **rickets** has been so called since the seventeenth century, but the origin of the word is uncertain. It may come, through its medical name *rachitis*, from *rakhis*, the Greek word for 'spine'. As with some of the other apparent plurals, one can say either 'rickets is . . .' or 'rickets are . . .'

influenza is the Italian word for 'influence', and the infection seems to have been thought of as a visitation caused by the malign influence of the stars. An epidemic of influenza started in Italy in the eighteenth century, and spread through Europe under its Italian name. In 1743 the *London Magazine* reported 'News from Rome of a contagious Distemper raging there, call'd the *Influenza*'. It became an English word, without italics. By 1801 Nelson was recording in a dispatch: 'In the *St George* we have got the Influenza.'

Though very contagious, it is not usually fatal. As Eliza Doolittle sensibly commented in Shaw's *Pygmalion*: 'My aunt died of influenza: so they said. But it's my belief they done the old woman in . . . Why should she die of influenza? She come through diphtheria right enough the year before.'

plague comes from the Latin *plaga*, 'a stroke or blow', and the word was used with that meaning in medieval English. In Wyclif's Bible of 1382, where God says in Ezekiel that 'I take away from thee the desire of thine eyes with a stroke', the last words are translated 'in plaga'. It also means an infestation or affliction, especially one regarded as a divine punishment; the ten plagues of Egypt, summoned up by Moses to force Pharaoh to let the Israelites go, included frogs, hail, and the turning of the Nile to blood. The word came to mean any pestilence, as it does in the Book of Common Prayer (1552), which prescribes a prayer 'In the tyme of any common plague or sickeness'. But from the sixteenth century onwards 'plague' was usually the oriental bubonic plague, which ravaged London for the last time in 1665, but had sporadically afflicted medieval Europe for centuries. The fourteenth-century Black Death was the same thing. The plague haunted the European imagination for centuries. Thomas Nashe wrote in the late sixteenth century:

> Rich men, trust not in wealth,
> Gold cannot buy you health;
> Physic himself must fade;
> All things to end are made;
> The plague full swift goes by;
> I am sick, I must die –
> *Lord, have mercy on us!*

The plague is now known to have been transmitted by fleas biting first infected rats and then human beings.

FOOD AND DRINK

This chapter would be intolerably long if we included everything we might be offered in a foreign restaurant! Omitted, therefore, are all comestibles such as moussaka and mozzarella which still belong too obviously to their country of origin. And certain edible fruits and vegetables such as the banana and potato come under 'Plants', though they could have been treated here. There are plenty left; the solid foods first:

curry is a Tamil word, *kari*, 'sauce', from south India. According to the *Hobson-Jobson* dictionary (1886) of Indian English, it first meant a spicy sauce used to give flavour to wheat cakes or boiled rice. Nowadays it usually means any sort of more or less spicy stew of meat, fish, or vegetables, usually though not always entailing chilli powder and turmeric. The British in India got used to it and began to demand it at home; in *Vanity Fair* 'Mrs Sedley had prepared a fine curry for her son', who had no doubt contracted the curry habit through his employment in the service of the East India Company, as Collector of Boggley Wollah in Bengal. (He very unkindly persuaded poor Becky Sharp to eat a chilli with it, which she thought was 'something cool, as its name imported'.)

This kind of curry is nothing to do with grooming a horse with a 'curry-comb', or with 'currying favour'. That 'curry' is purely European, and comes from Old French.

Another well-known dish from the Indian subcontinent is **kedgeree**, from the Hindi *khichṛī* and ultimately from Sanskrit. In India it was and is a strictly vegetarian food, a mixture of rice, pulses, butter, and perhaps onions, and under this name is very ancient: *Hobson-Jobson* records, charmingly, from 1443, 'The elephants of the palace are fed upon Kitchri.' But the traditional European breakfast dish always involves fish. Mrs Beeton gives as her ingredients cold white fish, boiled rice, hard-boiled eggs, butter, cayenne, and salt.

And **mulligatawny** soup is obviously Indian too. The Tamil word it comes from, *milagu-tannir*, means 'pepper-water'. The soup is indeed highly seasoned, but contains a lot of things beside pepper. (Mrs Beeton's recipe included rabbits, bacon, onions, and almonds.) Mulligatawny soup originated in Madras, so that British civil servants of the Madras presidency used to be called Mulligatawnies, or Mulls for short.

The condiments **chutney** and **ketchup** also come from the Orient: chutney from the Hindi *çatnī*, ketchup from Malay *kechap*, 'spiced fish sauce', and ultimately from Chinese. Both have of course been around in Britain for some time. In Dickens's *Barnaby Rudge* (1840) they ate 'some lamb chops (breaded, with plenty of ketchup)'. The Americans prefer the form **catsup**, though there is no suggestion that the stuff particularly appeals to cats.

We owe a surprising number of food words to the Portuguese, those indefatigable travellers and colonizers: **marmalade** comes to us through French from the Portuguese *marmelada*, 'quince jam', from two Greek words, *mela*, 'honey', and *melon*, 'apple'. The word has existed in English since the sixteenth century, but only in comparatively modern times has it come to imply oranges. British travellers on the Continent should be warned that *marmelade* in French simply means 'stewed fruit'.

Another Portuguese word is **molasses**, which is *melaço*, ultimately from *mel*, 'honey'. It means the syrup drained from raw sugar during refining, and has been an English word since the sixteenth century. Hakluyt's *Voyages* (1599) records, 'We spent heere very neere three moneths before we could get in our lading, which was Sugar, Dates, Almonds, and Malassos or sugar Syrrope.' The difference between molasses and treacle is a very technical one, and in fact Dr Johnson confused them, writing (1755): 'molosses, molasses. Treacle; the spume or scum of the juice of the sugar-cane.' Today, the Americans prefer the word molasses for the dark ingredient in treacle toffee.

But **treacle** itself is a more interesting word. It comes, through Latin, from the Greek *thēriakē*, 'antidote against venom', and under various spellings has been with us in pharmaceutical contexts since at least the eleventh century, meaning a medicine against snakebite and poison. In Chaucer's *Canterbury Tales* (*c.* 1386) the Host complains that one story was so sad it almost gave him a heart attack, and demands either 'triacle' = a dose of tonic, or a drink, to cheer him up. But when Mrs Squeers in Dickens's *Nicholas Nickleby* (1838) dosed the wretched boys at Dotheboys Hall with brimstone and treacle, the treacle was certainly what we would mean by the word. (Brimstone is sulphur.) By that time the modern sense of treacle was long established, and the stuff was familiar enough in Victorian nurseries for Lewis Carroll in *Alice in Wonderland* (1865) to have the Dormouse tell his story of three little sisters who lived at the bottom of a treacle-well.

Before we leave the sticky products of sugar cane, note that the familiar British golden **syrup**, a kind of pale treacle, gets its name through Old French from the Arabic *šarāb*, 'beverage'. That word too has been with us for a long time, and also at first in a medicinal sense. In *Othello* (1604) Iago comments,

> Not poppy, nor mandragora,
> Nor all the drowsy syrups of the world,
> Shall ever medicine thee to that sweet sleep
> Which thou owedst yesterday.

And about the same time, in Webster's *Duchess of Malfi* (1623), the doomed Duchess begs her executioners,

> I pray thee, look thou giv'st my little boy
> Some syrup for his cold . . .

Another substance for spreading on bread is **margarine**, with a curiously different and much more recent origin. An early nineteenth-century French chemist, Chevreuil, erroneously believed himself to have identified a fatty acid with a pearly appearance which he called *margarique*, from the Greek *margaron*, 'a pearl'. (It thus has the same root as the flower marguerite, the cocktail margarita, and the girl's name Margaret, although nowadays its first syllable is usually pronounced to rhyme with 'large'.) Chevreuil's fatty acid later turned out not to exist, but owing to a misapprehension the legal name margarine was patented, in 1873, for a butter substitute.

We come now to three sweets:

chocolate comes, through French and Spanish, from an Aztec word *chocolatl*. Chocolate first reached Europe as a beverage; in 1664 Samuel Pepys went 'to a Coffee-house, to drink jocolatte, very good'. We soon hear of it too as a solid confection. In 1720 Swift wrote in a letter, 'The chocolate is a present, madam, for Stella.' It is difficult now to imagine the world without chocolate, despite its exotic beginnings. As the soldier hero of Shaw's *Arms and the Man* (1898) remarked, 'What use are cartridges in battle? I always carry chocolate instead.'

candy comes from the Arabic *ḳand*, 'sugar'. In Britain it means crystallized sugar, or sugar spun into fluffy pink seaside candy-floss. In America it can apparently mean any kind of sweet, as it does in Ogden Nash's 'Reflections on ice-breaking' (1931):

> Candy
> Is dandy
> But liquor
> Is quicker.

And now a mystery, since nobody seems to know where **toffee** comes from. The word has existed since some time in the nineteenth century: in Thomas Hughes's *Tom Brown's School Days* (1857), for instance, 'it being only a step to the toffy shop, what could be more simple than to go there and fill their pockets . . .'

The Americans prefer to call it **taffy**, which is in fact the older form of the word. This has, of course, nothing to do with the rather offensive word Taffy, a Welshman.

★

A **biscuit** ought, from its derivation, to be cooked twice: Latin *bis*, 'twice', + *coctus*, 'baked'. The word seems to have first meant unleavened bread baked in the form of hard, dry cakes, to keep for as long as possible. In *As You Like It*, Jaques says that the fool's brain is 'as dry as the remainder biscuit after a voyage'. 'Captain's biscuit' was a superior form of this. As Thackeray wrote:

> There were three sailors of Bristol City
> Who took a boat and went to sea.
> But first with beef and captain's biscuits
> And pickled pork they loaded she . . .

Confusingly, in America a biscuit is more or less a bun or scone, and what the British call a biscuit they call a cracker or a cookie. In *Gone with the Wind*, the plantation owner's wife eats for supper 'golden-topped biscuits, breast of fried chicken and a yellow yam open and steaming'. Those biscuits must have been the ones defined in the Merriam–Webster American dictionary: 'a quick bread made in a small shape from dough that has been rolled and cut or dropped and that is raised in the baking by a leavening agent other than yeast'.

The next two kinds of biscuit are called after people. The *Bourbon* kings of France took their name from the castle and seigniory of Bourbon in central France and gave that name to the **Bourbon**, a kind of chocolate biscuit. That same French town must have given its name to Bourbon County in Kentucky, which in turn gave the name to Bourbon whiskey, distilled from maize and rye.

The **Garibaldi** currant biscuit, sometimes known as a 'squashed fly', is presumably called after Giuseppe *Garibaldi*, the nineteenth-century Italian revolutionary leader. It is not clear whether he ate them or liked them or even invented them. But there was great sympathy with his cause in Victorian England, where he was revered as a romantic hero.

The first **sandwich** was apparently eaten by John Montague, fourth Earl of Sandwich, a desperate character of the eighteenth century. (The earldom, by the way, is called after the town of Sandwich in Kent, not the town after the comestible; but Captain

Cook named the Sandwich Islands in the Pacific after the earl.) Besides being a member of the notorious Hellfire Club, and a deplorable First Lord of the Admiralty – 'For corruption and incapacity Sandwich's administration is unique in the history of the British navy,' says the *Encyclopaedia Britannica* – Sandwich was an impassioned gambler. He once spent twenty-four hours at the gaming-table, sustained only by slices of cold beef between slices of toast.

The word for this snack was new in the 1760s. Gibbon describes at that time a group of his acquaintances at a coffee-house as 'supping at little tables . . . upon a bit of cold meat, or a Sandwich'.

A sandwich now of course means anything 'sandwiched' between two other things, so that a sandwich man carries one advertisement board in front and another behind, and a sandwich course alternates periods of theoretical study with periods of work experience. Sandwiches need no longer be edible; a layer of material bonded between two layers of a different material is called a sandwich in aircraft construction and elsewhere. And they need no longer have a roof, as with the Scandinavian open sandwich.

Finally, two rather slangy words for food in general:

chow is a pidgin English word; that is, a word from the mixed language formerly used between Chinese and Europeans for business purposes. (Pidgin is a corruption of *business*.) It is a shortened form of chow-chow, known to many of us in Chinese restaurants as a dessert of mixed fruits in syrup. But 'chow' on its own came to be applied to food of any kind. *Hobson-Jobson* (1886) suggests that this sense has given its name to the Chinese breed of dog called a chow, 'from the erroneous impression that dogs form one of the principal items of a Chinaman's diet'. 'Chow' is also an abusive Australian word for a Chinaman. In 1921 *Chambers's Journal* reported, 'The pearling-crews can get from Japs and Chows all the drink they want.'

chow mein is fried noodles with a stew of meat and vegetables, and seems to have been first so called in America in the early twentieth century, when there were already Chinatowns in many major cities. Sinclair Lewis in *Main Street* (1920) refers to 'the golden fried noodles of the chow mein'.

   nosh is Yiddish, from the German *naschen*, 'to nibble on the sly'. This German sense is preserved chiefly in America, for the nibbling of small titbits between meals. In *The Joys of Yiddish* (1968) Leo Rosten explains, 'Many delicatessen counters display plates with small slices of salami, or pieces of halvah, with a legend affixed to a toothpick: "Have a nosh."' In Britain, though, nosh is just food, or a meal, and a nosh-up is a good lavish one. Thus, in Ruth Rendell's *A Guilty Thing Surprised* (1970) a hostess presiding over 'a table loaded with food, roast fowls, cold joints, a whole salmon', comments, 'If you're sure that's enough nosh.'

And now, some drinks:

   alcohol is Arabic, from *al*, 'the', and *kuhl*, 'kohl', a black powder used as eye make-up. (This Arabic *al* for 'the' lurks in several English words; particularly those to do with the learned sciences, such as algebra and alchemy, which reached us through the Moors in Spain.) From other senses in early chemistry, alcohol came to mean spirits produced by distillation, and then any intoxicating drink whether distilled or fermented. Dr Johnson (1755) is rather technical about it: 'alcohol, an Arabick term used by chymists for a high rectified dephlegmated spirit of wine, or for any thing reduced into an impalpable powder'. The technical senses are, of course, still with us today; but that is not what Andrew Undershaft meant in Shaw's *Major Barbara* (1907) when he commented, 'Alcohol . . . enables Parliament to do things at eleven at night that no sane person would do at eleven in the morning,' or Bertie Wooster, who revealed in Wodehouse's *The Inimitable Jeeves* (1923), 'It was my Uncle George who discovered that alcohol was a food well in advance of medical thought.'

   While we are on the subject of alcoholic drinks, **whisky** is Gaelic, from *usquebaugh*, *uisge beatha*, 'water of life'. The word exactly corresponds, when one comes to think of it, to the Scandinavian **aquavit**, which means 'water of life' too. Traditionally the Scottish drink is whisky while the Irish is whiskey, and the latter has become the standard American spelling. Robert Burns, who ought to know, wrote 'Freedom and Whisky gang thegither!'

But **brandy** is Dutch, from an earlier Dutch form *brandewijn*, 'burnt (= distilled) wine'. It is pleasant that an older English form 'brandewine' gave its name to the Brandywine river in the American state of Delaware. Tolkien presumably borrowed this splendid river name for a river in *The Lord of the Rings* (1954).

gin is short for *Geneva*, but it has nothing to do with the Swiss city of that name. The drink called geneva was first made in Holland, and was flavoured with (though *not* distilled from) juniper berries; *genever* is the Dutch for juniper. It was often called geneva, or Hollands Geneva, even when it was made in Britain. In the reign of George II gin drinking became a public menace. Pope explains in a note (1738) to one of his poems, 'A spirituous liquor, the exorbitant use of which had almost destroyed the lowest rank of the People till it was restrained by an act of Parliament in 1736.' At about the same time, Hogarth made the same point in his two famous drawings contrasting the health and prosperity of 'Beer Street' with the disease and poverty of 'Gin Lane'. There, the drunken populace pawn their tools and household goods, a woman drops her baby, a corpse is being coffined, a suicide hangs from a beam.

Cheap gin must have been extremely nasty. In 1751 Sir John Hill recorded in his *Materia Medica*: 'At present only a better kind is distilled [*sic*] from the juniper-berry: what is commonly sold is made with no better an ingredient than oil of turpentine, put into the still, with a little common salt, and the coarsest spirit they have, which is drawn off much below proof strength.'

It is only more recently that gin has become such a universal party drink. As Douglas Adams suggests in his *Restaurant at the End of the Universe* (1980): 'Something like 85 per cent of all known worlds in the Galaxy, be they primitive or highly advanced, have invented a drink called jynnan tonnyx, or gee-N'N-T'N-ix, or jinond-o-nicks, or any one of a thousand or more variations on the same phonetic theme.'

And **punch** probably comes from the Hindi *pāc*, 'five', from the number of its ingredients: wine or spirits, sugar, lemon or lime juice, spice, and water. The word seems to have been current in India by the seventeenth century, and brought back thence to England. Evelyn records in his *Diary* (1662), 'I accompanied the Duke to an East India vessell that lay at Blackwall, where we had entertainment . . . Amongst other spirituous drinks, as punch, etc. they gave us . . .' The eponymous hero of Defoe's *Robinson Crusoe* (1719) records ruefully, 'We went the old way of all Sailors, the Punch was made, and I was made drunk with it.'

When the magazine *Punch* began publication in 1847, it got its name, not so much from the Punch of Punch and Judy, who appeared on Richard Doyle's first cover, as from a humorous allusion to the name of its first editor, Mark Lemon, since lemons are an ingredient of punch.

hooch first meant the liquor made by the *Hoochinoo*, a small tribe who lived on Admiralty Island, Alaska. One traveller records how they 'distilled a villainous compound from molasses, yeast, berries, sugar, or other compounds'. The word came to be used for any nasty cheap spirits, particularly when illicitly distilled.

plonk, cheap wine, is probably a corruption of the French *vin blanc*, 'white wine', the only objection to this idea being that plonk is usually red. The word arose in Australia soon after the First World War. Perhaps we must imagine Australian soldiers drinking in French cafés on the Somme?

grog is said to be short for *grogram*, and a certain eighteenth-century Admiral Vernon had the nickname Old Grog, from the grogram cloak in which he walked the decks in rough weather. He was famed for his order, dated August 1740, that the sailors' rum rations should be diluted with water instead of being served neat. A rhyme of 1781 celebrates the event:

> A mighty bowl on deck he drew,
> And filled it to the brink;
> Such drank the Burford's gallant crew,
> And such the gods shall drink,
> The sacred robe which Vernon wore

> Was drenched within the same;
> And hence his virtues guard our shore,
> And Grog derives its name.

Grog is thus traditionally rum and water, or more recently a mixture of water with any spirit. 'Mix me a grog,' said Michael Finsbury in Robert Louis Stevenson's 'Wrong Box'; 'Heaven forgive you, it's a lemonade! ... Here, put some gin in this!' But the Australians and New Zealanders use the word for any alcoholic drink, including beer.

The first meaning of 'groggy' was 'drunk', though it now means simply dazed and tottering. And a grog-blossom is a drunkard's red nose.

sherbet and **shrub** (= the drink, not the bush) both come from the Arabic *šariba*, 'to drink'. As romantically drunk in the *Arabian Nights*, sherbet was a soft drink (appropriately for Muslim countries) made of sweetened and diluted fruit juice, sometimes cooled with snow. The word has since been variously used for fizzy lemonade powder, and (particularly in America) for water ices. Richard Hoggart wrote nostalgically in *The Uses of Literacy* (1957) of the 'sherbet-fountain', a bag of fizzy powder to be sucked through an attached stick of liquorice: 'The boy's odder pleasures of taste ... sherbet-fountains, monkey nuts and aniseed balls ...' In colloquial Australian use, though, sherbet is beer.

And **shrub**, too, may or may not be alcoholic. Its first use goes back to the eighteenth century, when it seems to have been a mixture of rum and sweetened lemon juice; in fact what today we might call a daiquiri. Sailors drank it, making it presumably by mixing the naval rum ration with the lemons provided against scurvy. But the Americans also use the word for a soft drink made of raspberry juice.

tea is the Chinese *te*, which reached English through Dutch. The leaves were first imported into Europe in the seventeenth century. Pepys was drinking it by 1660: 'I did send for a cup of tee (a China drink) of which I never had drunk before.' (An alternative Chinese word *cha*, from another dialect, accounts for the British slang word **char**, which reached us only in the late nineteenth century, through Hindi, from the army serving in India. It has of course nothing to do with the job of charring as a char-woman; that is quite a different word, related to *chore*.) Dr Johnson, who was much addicted to tea, defines it (1755) as 'A Chinese plant, of which the infusion has lately been much drunk in Europe.' Johnson's dictionary does not attempt to describe pronunciation, beyond marking the stressed syllable of multi-syllable words; but at the time at which he wrote, he very probably pronounced 'tea' as 'tay'. This is evident from rhymes of the period: when the heroine of *The Rape of the Lock* (1711) visits Hampton Court, Pope apostrophizes the place:

> Here thou, great Anna! whom three realms obey,
> Dost sometimes counsel take – and sometimes tea.

But tea is a meal as well as a drink, particularly in Britain, and has been since the late eighteenth century. It was a meal in Belloc's 'Henry King' (1907):

> Breakfast, Dinner, Lunch, and Tea
> Are all the human frame requires . . .

and in Rupert Brooke's 'The Old Vicarage, Grantchester' (1915):

> Stands the Church clock at ten to three?
> And is there honey still for tea?

There is always some confusion, partly social and partly geographi-cal, about whether an invitation to tea means cakes and sandwiches at about half-past four or – as it probably does in the north – a solid cooked evening meal at about six.

cocoa is a confusing word. It is a version of *cacao*, the name in the Central American language Nahuatl of the tree (*uatl* means 'tree' in Nahuatl) from whose seed pods it is made. So is chocolate. Cocoa is nothing to do with **coca**, which is the South American shrub that cocaine comes from and whose name comes from *cuca* in the Peruvian language Quechua. Neither of them has anything to do with **coconuts**, the nuts of the **coco** palm tree; that word is

Portuguese and Spanish, and *coco* means a 'grimace' or 'bogeyman', because that is what someone thought the three holes at the base of the shell looked like. Finally, the proprietary drink **Coca-Cola** has nothing much to do with any of them.

Chesterton, who apparently disapproved of all soft drinks, thought cocoa was the worst of the lot. He wrote in *The Flying Inn* (1914):

> Tea, although an Oriental,
> Is a gentleman at least;
> Cocoa is a cad and coward,
> Cocoa is a vulgar beast.

CLOTHS

Many fabrics are called after the place where they were first made. The bizarre variety of their origins illustrates particularly well the richness of the English language.

First come several kinds of cotton or linen cloth:

muslin comes, through the French *mousseline*, from the name of the city Mosul in what is now Iraq. It has meant a fabric of some sort since the Middle Ages: Marco Polo in the thirteenth century referred to silk and cloth of gold as Mosolins. In more recent British use, however, 'muslin' has usually meant a light cotton cloth, imported into Europe since the late seventeenth century from various parts of India. In Jane Austen's *Northanger Abbey* (1818) Henry Tilney boasts, 'I gave but five shillings a yard for it, and a true India muslin.' As with most fabrics, a 'muslin' may mean a muslin dress: Thackeray wrote in *Vanity Fair* (1848), 'She insisted upon Rebecca accepting . . . a sweet sprigged muslin, which was too small for her now.' ('Sprigged' muslin was ornamented with a woven or embroidered pattern of little plant sprays.)

In America, the word is also used for quite coarse cotton fabric, suitable for shirts, sheets, and so on; yet another possible cause of international misunderstanding.

calico derives from *Calicut*, a coastal city of Malabar in south India, famous for weaving cotton and an early trading station of the East India Company. (The city is now called Kozhikode.) This word came to be applied particularly to white unprinted cotton of medium weight, imported from the East from the sixteenth century onwards. Pepys wrote in 1666, 'Flags, which I had bought for the Navy, of calico.' It was a cheap cloth, often associated with poverty. In Jane Austen's *Mansfield Park* (1814) Mrs Norris nags her poor little niece Fanny: 'If you have no work of your own, I can supply you from the poor basket. There is all the new calico, that was bought last week, not touched yet.'

In America, though, calico is any cheap brightly printed cotton cloth, which accounts for the adjectival use of 'calico' to describe a piebald or spotted animal. A calico cat has black and orange patches: is in fact tortoiseshell.

chintz comes from the plural of the Hindi *chīṇt*, and is printed Indian calico, or nowadays usually a glazed cotton furnishing fabric. It has spawned the curious adjective 'chintzy', which can mean either cosy and homely in a suburban way or (more in American use) cheap, tawdry, or stingy. In 1932, John Betjeman has a nurse address a dying woman thus:

> And 'Tea!' she said in a tiny voice
> 'Wake up! It's nearly *five*.'
> Oh! Chintzy, chintzy cheeriness,
> Half dead and half alive!

madras, naturally, is named after the south Indian city of *Madras*. Madras cotton is typically woven in plain patterns of stripes or checks, suitable for shirts and dresses, and 'bleeds' when laundered.

The **dungaree** that dungarees are made of is another cotton cloth, a coarse, usually blue, denim. The word comes from the Hindi *dungrī*. But **denim** is *de Nîmes*, from the town in the south of France. Though we still use the word for a hard-wearing cotton fabric, it is also common today in the plural, meaning denim jeans or overalls. And **jeans**, by the way, are so called because of a cotton cloth called jean, once made at *Genoa* in Italy, though now they are more typically made of denim.

seersucker is usually light cotton, though it can be linen or synthetic. The crucial fact about it is its weave, with alternate stripes puckered, which makes it suitable for men's uncrushable hot-weather suits. The word comes from the Persian *šīr-o-šakar*, 'milk and sugar'.

lawn probably comes from *Laon* in France, and has always been a superior fine linen or cotton fabric. In *The Winter's Tale* the pedlar Autolycus advertises 'Lawn as white as driven snow', and in his 'Eve of St Mark' (1829) Keats wrote:

> From plaited lawn-frill, fine and thin,
> She lifted up her soft warm chin.

Since bishops wore lawn sleeves, the word has long had an episcopal flavour. Pope used it like that in his *Moral Essays* (1782):

> 'Tis from high life high characters are drawn;
> A saint in crape is twice a saint in lawn.

buckram came to us through Old French, perhaps from *Bokhara* in central Asia. The word has been with us since the Middle Ages, but has come to mean cloth stiffened for collars and linings. Its chief literary association is the momentous scene in *King Henry IV Part 1*, when Falstaff fraudulently complains of having been attacked by 'two rogues in buckram suits', who gradually increase to four, seven, nine, and finally eleven, to be reinforced by 'three misbegotten knaves in Kendal green'.

lisle is from *Lisle*, the old spelling of *Lille* in France. It is the cotton thread which was used for cheaper stockings before they were all made of nylon.

cambric was first made at *Cambrai* in northern France. This fine white material seems to have been much associated with superior handkerchiefs.

gauze gets its name from *Gaza*, in south Palestine. This very thin, transparent fabric seems to have been with us since at least the sixteenth century, perhaps through the influence of the Crusades. The word is also used for a slight haze, so that the innermost and faintest ring of Saturn is the 'gauze ring'.

damask is called after the city of *Damascus*, the capital of Syria. This figured silk or linen cloth, originally produced there, was known very early in England. In the *Paston Letters* (1473) somebody was lucky enough to acquire 'a newe vestment off whyght damaske'.

And finally **gingham**, which reached English through Dutch, from the Malay *ginggang* meaning 'striped'. It is indeed a usually checked or striped cotton cloth, and appears to have had this name since the sixteenth century and to have been an important item in the Indian trade.

Some words for silks are:

shantung, which comes from the name of the Chinese province *Shantung*. Since the late nineteenth century the word has been used in English for a silk cloth with a slightly rough surface produced by the inclusion of wild silk yarns; and **tussore** or (chiefly American) tussah or tusser is the silk, originally brown, of a particular kind of silkworm called *tasar* in Hindi, from the Sanskrit word for a shuttle – probably because of the shape of its cocoon.

A **bandanna** is a large, brightly patterned, often spotted, cotton or silk handkerchief, probably from the Hindi *bāndhnū*, tie-dyed cloth. (Tie-dying is the process of tying knots in a fabric before dying, to produce a pattern of undyed areas.) Trollope in *The Last Chronicle of Barset* (1866) wrote of Toogood 'wiping his eyes with a large red bandana handkerchief'. Bandannas were very popular with the Victorian working class. In his *London Life and the London Poor* (1851) Henry Mayhew wrote:

Men, women, boys and girls, all have a passion for these articles. The [costermonger] who does not wear his silk neckerchief – his 'King's-man' as it is called – is known to be in desperate circumstances; the inference being that it has gone to supply the morning's stock-money. A yellow flower on a green ground, or a red and blue pattern, is at present greatly in vogue. The women wear their kerchiefs tucked-in under their gowns, and the men have theirs wrapped loosely round the neck, with the ends hanging over their waistcoats.

And **tulle** is a soft, silky net, first made at *Tulle* in the south of France.

Some woollen fabrics are:

cashmere. It was originally wool from the soft woolly undercoat of the Kashmir goat, which first became familiar here in the form of cashmere shawls, brought or sent home from India for English ladies. The soft fine wool of the modern cashmere sweater is no longer usually of Eastern origin.

worsted is a long-staple yarn or fabric from *Worstead* in Norfolk, a centre of the medieval wool industry. This word has been with us since medieval times. One of these early wool merchants had this rhyme set in his window:

> I thanke God and ever shall
> It is the sheep hath payed for all.

The Friar in Chaucer's *Canterbury Tales* (*c.* 1386) was so smart and prosperous that

> He was lyk a maister or a pope;
> Of double worstede was his semycope.

And in 1962 Len Deighton was writing in *The Ipcress File* 'I struggled into the dark worsted and my only establishment tie.'

angora comes from *Angora* in Turkey, now called Ankara. It was originally made only of the silky hair of the angora goat or rabbit, but the rabbit hair is now usually mixed with sheep's wool. It is also the name of a kind of fluffy cat.

And finally:

The stuffing and insulating material **kapok** gets its name from the Malay *kāpoq*. It is the silky floss round the seeds of the ceiba tree, and it keeps you warm. In *Spy Story* (1974) Len Deighton wrote of 'kapok-lined white snow-suits'.

jute comes, through the Bengali *jhōṭo*, from a Sanskrit word meaning 'braid of hair'. It is the fibre of two Indian plants of the linden family, used for sacking and twine, and has been an important export to the West since the early nineteenth century, processed in Britain as well as in India. The resultant coarse sacking is **gunny**, from the Hindi *gōnī*, a sack; but another word for it is **hessian**, called after *Hesse* in Germany.

GARMENTS

Here the word more usually comes from the country where the thing was first worn, with no particular reference to its manufacture. These are names of things English-speaking people might actually wear. We do not include 'ethnic' garments that have remained merely ethnic.

trousers are Irish and Gaelic, from *triubhas*, which used to be a singular word. They have become plural, perhaps through being, as the child said, 'singular at the top and plural lower down'. In modern times they were first worn by sailors, and only replaced breeches as general men's wear after about 1820.

While we are considering that part of the body, **jodhpurs** for riding are called after *Jodhpur*, a former princely state in northwestern India. They are imitated from the traditional style of Indian trousers, baggy at the top and close-fitting below the knee, and have caught on – only in this century – as a comfortable and cheaper alternative to the conventional riding-breeches, which entail expensive knee-length boots. In 1931 *The Times* described the present Queen as a little girl dressed for riding, 'with her fair curls shining and wearing a yellow jumper pulled down over her jodhpurs'.

pants are short for *pantaloons*; and pantaloons come by a long route from St Pantaleone, a patron saint of physicians, in Asia Minor. He became popular with the seafaring Venetians – perhaps because his name sounds like 'all-lion', and the Lion of St Mark was their totem animal. They gave the name to Pantaloon, a stupid old man with spectacles, slippers, and baggy trousers, the traditional clown of Italian comedy. Shakespeare uses it like that in *As You Like It*:

> The sixth age shifts
> Into the lean and slippered pantaloon,
> With spectacles on nose and pouch on side;
> His youthful hose, well saved, a world too wide
> For his shrunk shank . . .

Shakespeare had in fact already noticed the 'bagginess'.

The word came to mean trousers, called after this Italian clown, some time after the Restoration. Defoe used it in *Robinson Crusoe* (1719), when Crusoe made himself 'a pair of open-kneed breeches . . . made of the skin of an old he-goat, whose hair hung down such a length on either side that like pantaloons it reached to the middle of my legs'.

pyjamas come from the Urdu and Hindi *pae*, 'leg', + *jāma*, 'clothing'. They consisted originally of just loose trousers, a Muslim garment adopted by the Europeans in India; then the word came to be used for the familiar suit of trousers and jacket.

The Americans spell it 'pajamas'. One must imagine this spelling when Groucho Marx recounts in the film *Animal Crackers* (1930): 'One morning I shot an elephant in my pajamas. How he got into my pajamas I'll never know.'

Two cold-weather garments for the top half of the body were first worn by Eskimos: **anorak** from the Greenland Eskimo word *anoraq*, for a hooded weatherproof jacket or smock, first noticed as part of Eskimo costume and later adopted for mountaineering and skiing; and the very similar **parka**, which is so called in the language of the Aleutian islands to the west of Alaska.

The **poncho** is another garment from the New World, but from rather warmer latitudes. This sort of blanket cloak with a hole for the head comes to us through Spanish from the South American Indian language Araucanian: *pontho*, 'woollen fabric'. The word has been recorded in English since the early eighteenth century, but the garment caught on outside Latin America much more recently. In *The Drunken Forest* (1956) Gerald Durrell still had to explain it: 'I found him clad in pyjamas and a *poncho*, that useful Argentine garment that resembles a blanket with a hole in the middle through which you stick your head.'

The **jersey** and the **guernsey**, of course, get their names from their respective Channel Islands. Jersey is much the older word, as it was used to mean any knitted garment, or just woollen fabric, before it came in the nineteenth century to mean a sweater. (Mary Queen of Scots is described as wearing jersey stockings.) In *Tom Brown's School Days* (1857) each house at Rugby 'has its own uniform of cap and jersey, of some lively colour'. The distinctive thick blue woollen guernsey is mentioned about the same time as being worn by sailors. In Australia, though, a guernsey is a football shirt, so that to 'get a guernsey', which originally meant to be picked for the football team, now means to succeed and get recognition.

The word **cagoule** is French. Although in English it means much the same sort of hooded windproof garment as the anorak or parka, in French, confusingly, a *cagoule* is just a hood or cowl, more or less what we would call a balaclava.

The **balaclava** itself, of course, is called after the battle of *Balaclava* in 1854, in the Crimean war. That particular war seems to have given rise to other words for garments that keep you warm, owing to the ferocious weather conditions of the Crimea in winter.

The woolly **cardigan** derives from the 7th Earl of *Cardigan*, who led the ill-fated charge of the Light Brigade. And the then British commander, Lord *Raglan*, gave his name to the characteristic **raglan** sleeves of an overcoat, running up to the neck rather than being set in at the shoulder; perhaps because in very cold weather there is more room to wear other clothes underneath.

But **wellingtons** date from an older war, being called after the first Duke of *Wellington*: 'He that gained a hundred fights/ Nor ever lost an English gun', as Tennyson put it. He gave his name to the Wellington boot immediately after his victory in 1815 at Waterloo. They seem to have been first a sort of cavalry boot, higher in front than at the back, and only later to have become the familiar British waterproof rubber or plastic wellies.

puttees are from the Hindi word *paṭṭī*, a bandage or strip of cloth, and were originally long cloth strips wound spirally round the leg from ankle to knee. The practice of wearing them seems to have been introduced from the Himalayas, and taken up by European sportsmen and soldiers in the nineteenth century. As part of army uniform they appear in photographs from the trenches of the First World War, where they kept out the appalling mud; but their wearers report that they were difficult to put on, being sloppy if too loosely wrapped and restricting the circulation if too tight. The cloth strips were superseded in army use by gaiters with straps, also called puttees, which fulfil the same purpose of something to tuck the bottoms of the trouser legs into.

Before we leave these military matters, one might note that **khaki** is an Urdu word, *ḳākī*, meaning dust-coloured. The colour came to replace military red in India by the middle of the nineteenth century, and by the end of the century was the standard field uniform colour of the British army in the South African war. Although it can still mean no more than the colour (as in the case of the four children in the limerick who on orthodox Mendelian lines were 'one black and one white and two khaki') the word has come to be associated so closely with the army that an election swayed by militaristic hysteria has been called a 'khaki election'. The opposite, so to speak, of khaki in its military sense is **mufti**, for civilian clothes worn by someone who is usually in uniform. This mysterious word may come from the Arabic *muftī*, a Muslim priest or legal expert. Somerset Maugham in *Cakes and Ale* (1930) wrote 'He looked a little like a dean in mufti on his summer holiday in Switzerland.'

And now some footwear:

brogues are from *bróg*, Gaelic and Irish, 'shoe'. In early times they were a somewhat primitive kind of Celtic shoe, made of untanned leather: it sounds smelly. In his *Journey to the Western Islands of Scotland* (1775) Dr Johnson remarks 'In Sky I first observed the use of brogues, a kind of artless Shoe.' The other meaning of brogue, an Irish (or occasionally Scots) accent, is mysterious. It is tempting to believe, as the *Oxford Dictionary* suggests, that brogue may be the way people talk who wear brogues, or who call their shoes brogues, but there is no evidence for this. Another suggestion is that the word may come from the Irish Gaelic *barrog*, a 'hold' or 'bond'. There the matter rests.

moccasins are another sort of early footwear, but here the word comes from Algonquian, a North American Indian language. The word was used as early as the seventeenth century by speakers of English settled in America. These soft slippers are easily assembled by amateurs: in 1965 the New Zealand *Listener* referred to them as 'the shearer's home-made footwear, usually made of sacking or felt'.

gauntlet is like brogue, another case of two words with the same spelling. As a glove, it is fairly predictably related to the French *gant*, 'glove', and this is the sense implied when someone challenges an adversary by 'throwing down the gauntlet'. But when we are subjected to the disagreeable punishment of 'running the gauntlet', either figuratively or in the literal sense of having to run between two lines of people who each hit us as we pass, we are involved with a quite different word that comes from the Swedish *gatlopp*, which means 'lane, course'. This word turned into 'gauntlet' by the process technically called 'folk etymology', the adapting of a strange word to make it sound more familiar, as when some people call asparagus 'sparrow-grass'.

For two items of headgear we return to the East:

turban comes, through Turkish, from the Persian *dulband*, and of course first meant the traditional men's headdress of a strip of cloth wound round either a cap or one's head, as worn by Muslims and Sikhs. A similar object has been fashionable wear for women at various times. Before Waterloo, Mrs Major O'Dowd in Thackeray's *Vanity Fair* wore 'her turban and bird of Paradise', and Miss Matty in Mrs Gaskell's *Cranford* wished she had one too: 'I should have liked . . . something more like the turbans Miss Betty Barker tells me Queen Adelaide wears.' And as photographs of the period show, a simplified sort of turban was standard wear among women factory-workers and others during the Second World War.

And what of that romantic, nostalgic, or absurd (whichever way you look at it) empire-builder's hat, the **sola topee**? In the first place, the word is not 'solar' and does not mean 'sun'. This hat is made of the pith of a plant called *solā* in Urdu and Bengali, but it is often misspelt. Noël Coward got it wrong in his unforgettable 'Mad Dogs and Englishmen':

> It's such a surprise for the Eastern eyes to see,
> That though the English are effete
> They're quite impervious to heat.
> When the white man rides every native hides in glee,
> Because the simple creatures hope he
> Will impale his solar topee on a tree . . .

The **shawl** and the **sash** come from the Persian *šāl* and the Arabic *šāš*. Both are essentially just strips of cloth, and today we would think of a sash as worn by women, and a shawl by either women or babies; but in the Orient, where they originated, men wore them too, using the sash as a turban cloth. The sash was part of a British army officer's uniform until this century; and in Margaret Mitchell's *Gone with the Wind*, Scarlett O'Hara gives 'a long yellow sash, made of thick China silk and edged with heavy fringe', to the man she loves, when he goes off to rejoin the Confederate army in the American Civil War.

And, finally, a **cravat** is a Croatian. The Croatian mercenaries in the French army wore cravats, and *Hrvat* is their name for themselves in their own language. This linen neckcloth became fashionable in seventeenth-century France for both men and women, and in Britain by the time of the Restoration. People who were hanged were said to wear a hempen cravat.

DWELLINGS AND EDIFICES

bungalow is a Hindi word *baṅglā*, which originally meant 'belonging to Bengal'. The word was used when Europeans in India began to build 'Bengal-style' houses, with only one storey and often a veranda all round. It is interesting that although an English bungalow today has no upstairs, the word is used in modern India for any free-standing detached house, and is rather prestigious.

The **veranda** round the bungalow, a pleasant place to shelter from the tropical sun, reached Europe as a word because of the experience of the English in India. It is of mysterious origin, since though there is certainly a Hindi word *varandā*, that itself apparently comes through Portuguese from Spanish. In Australia 'veranda' means a roofed area on the pavement outside a shop, and also an open outside gallery upstairs, as if for Juliet's balcony scene.

A **window** is an eye of the wind: Old Norse *vindr*, 'wind', + *auga*, 'eye'. As the word comes from the cold latitudes of Scandinavia, and as there were windows in buildings for centuries before glazing came in, the idea of 'wind' is entirely suitable. But nowadays we often mean the glass in the window, rather than the hole which it fills, that being what you break when you break a window. Or a window may be the display area behind a glass shop-window, as in the fifties song, 'How much is that doggie in the window?'

The word has since developed various technical senses, an up-to-date one being in space technology; a 'launch window' is the period of time when the positions of the planets make it possible to launch a spacecraft.

The **attic** of a house comes, by a curious route, from the Greek

Attikos, 'Athenian'. That is how Keats used the word in his 'Ode on a Grecian Urn' (1819):

> O Attic shape! Fair Attitude! with brede
> Of marble men and maidens overwrought . . .

In Greek classical architecture the attic was a small row of columns placed, in the Athenian manner, above the main ones in a façade; then the word came to mean the space behind those columns, and then the top storey of a house.

A **mansion** was originally just a place to live, which is what it means in St John's Gospel: 'In my Father's house are many mansions', and in Milton's 'Ode on the Morning of Christ's Nativity' (1629):

> And Hell itself will pass away
> And leave her dolorous mansions to the peering day.

More recently (1933), W. B. Yeats wrote:

> Love has pitched his mansion in
> The place of excrement.

It comes from the Latin *mansio*, 'a staying'. Later a mansion came to be a large, dignified sort of house, such as that inhabited by Charles Augustus Fortescue in Belloc's *Cautionary Tales* (1939):

> He thus became immensely Rich,
> And built the Splendid Mansion which
> Is called 'The Cedars, Muswell Hill',
> Where he resides in Affluence still . . .

Even grander, **palace** comes from the Latin *palatium*, which was originally the name of one of the seven hills of Rome, the Mons Palatinus. The Emperor Augustus lived there, and the palace of the Caesars finally covered the whole hill. The word came to mean a royal residence in several European languages as well as English.

We use the word in that royal sense, of course, as with the Palace of Westminster – a royal residence from Canute's day; but it also means the house of a British bishop or archbishop. (Consider, for instance, Mrs Proudie's strictures on her new home when she and the bishop moved in in Trollope's *Barchester Towers* (1857): 'Surely the palace should have been fitted through with pipes for gas, and hot water too.') And it can mean any splendid mansion, such as the Duke of Marlborough's Blenheim Palace; or, from the Crystal Palace onwards, a spacious exhibition hall or place of entertainment.

In modern British use 'The Palace' often means the monarchy. And a 'palace revolution' is the fairly peaceful overthrow of a government by senior officials or the ruler's own intimates.

Coming down now to some smaller buildings, **kiosk** is a Turkish word, *kiūshk*, 'pavilion'. In Turkey and Persia they were ornamental pillared summer-houses, rather like a bandstand. The word was taken up in Europe for an open structure selling newspapers or tickets, and is used particularly in Australia for a building where refreshments are sold in a public place, such as a hospital or zoo. It seems to be only in Britain that a closed telephone box is a kiosk.

A **shack**, though, may get its name from the Aztec word *xacatli*, 'wooden hut'. In any case, the word originated in America and Canada; as did the verb to **shack up**, 'to lodge temporarily' and thence 'to cohabit sexually'. In 1957, for instance, the *Economist* referred to 'Private Gerard's marriage to the Japanese girl with whom he had been "shacked up"'.

Some more dwellings of the New World are the **tepee** and the **wigwam**: the first from the Dakota word *tīpī*, *ti* 'to dwell', and *pi* 'to use for'; the second from the Algonquian *wikiwam*, 'their house'. Both are constructed on a framework of poles, but strictly speaking the conical kind covered with skins is a tepee, while a wigwam is the shape of an inverted cup and is often covered with matting. Yet as wigwam is the better-known word, gardening books often advise one to plant climbing things such as beans or sweet peas on a conical 'wigwam' arrangement of canes.

To move further north, the dome-shaped snow **igloo** comes from the Eskimo word for 'house'. Here it is apparently the shape that has caught the imagination of the world, so that one now hears of igloos made of very diverse materials. *Jane's Freight Con-*

tainers (1969) illustrates 'a moulded fibreglass igloo unit as used by Delta Airlines'.

The obscure word **pagoda** has one of two origins. It is a foreigners' corruption either of the Hindi *bhagavat*, 'holy', or of the Persian *butkada*, 'idol temple'. The second explanation is more likely, since the Portuguese would have picked up the word from the Muslims with whom they chiefly had to deal when they first reached India; and the two meanings are amusingly opposite, since the Muslims would have despised and rejected any material representation of a god. Foreigners came to use the word about the temples of India, Java, and the Malay peninsula, and particularly with reference to the curly-roofed, tapering, many-storeyed towers of China and Japan: the pagoda in Kew Gardens is typical.

Pagoda was also the name of a south Indian gold coin, from which came the term 'to shake the pagoda-tree'. This meant to make a fortune rapidly in India, as many of the early servants of the East India Company did if they survived the climate.

The grandest edifice in this list is the **cathedral**, which comes through Latin from the Greek *kathedra*, 'seat'. A cathedral, the principal church of a diocese, contains the throne of a bishop or archbishop. When the Pope makes a pronouncement **ex cathedra**, from his official seat of office, he is said to be infallible, speaking in his pontifical capacity as the successor and representative of St Peter. The expression is used of other dogmatic assertions: in *Rob Roy* (1818) Scott refers to 'the punctilios exacted by Owen in their business transactions – for he was a great lover of form, more especially when he could dictate it *ex cathedra . . .*'

FURNITURE

The most interesting words here all seem to be for things you can lie or sprawl on:

A **sofa** is, according to Dr Johnson, 'a splendid seat covered with carpets'. This splendid seat comes ultimately from the Arabic *ṣuffa*. In those Eastern countries where the word originated, a sofa was a raised part of the floor, made comfortable for sitting on with carpets and cushions. That was the form in which Samuel Purchas first saw one, and recorded it in his *Pilgrimage* (1613): 'A sofa spread with very sumptuous Carpets of Gold ... on which the Grand Signior sitteth'.

The sofa as we know it came into England in the eighteenth century; when William Cowper wrote in *The Task* (1784):

> Thus first necessity invented stools,
> Convenience next suggested elbow-chairs,
> And luxury th'accomplished Sofa last.

divan comes through Arabic from the Persian *dīvān*, which was not a piece of furniture at all. The earliest meaning, in the related spelling 'dewan', was of a collection of writings, an account book, or a fiscal register. (This gave rise to the French *douane* and Italian *dogana*, for the Customs.) A dewan then came to be the Prime Minister of an Indian princely state; Mahatma Gandhi's father held this office. The same word meant an oriental council chamber. Here the ruler would sit to hold public audience on a raised platform or dais made comfortable with cushions, and that is what our idea of a divan comes from.

To the Victorians, a divan was still often a room rather than a couch. A cigar divan was a place where you could go to smoke, lounging presumably on comfortable sofas.

cot, in the furniture sense, is another Oriental word. The Hindi *khāṭ*, from Sanskrit, means any kind of light bedstead or couch, and the word was so used by Europeans in India from the early seventeenth century. It particularly applied to a piece of barrack furniture for soldiers, or to a swinging bed, a hammock in fact, on board ship. In American use a cot is still what the British would call a camp-bed, but in British English it now really means only a baby's bed, with high sides to stop the child from falling out. Hence, 'cot-death' is the unexplained death of a sleeping baby.

hammock, however, comes from the New World. The Spanish word *hamaca* derives from Carib, a language of the West Indies. It was used, by the sixteenth century, for the swinging contraption that sailors sleep in: Sir Walter Ralegh in his *Discoverie of the Empyre of Guiana* (1596) describes how 'They lay each of them in a cotten Hamaca.'

A dead sailor could be sewn into his canvas hammock and weighted down with cannon-balls before being committed to the deep. That is what is going on in Sir Henry Newbolt's patriotic poem 'Drake's Drum':

> Drake he's in his hammock till the great Armadas come,
> (Capten, art tha sleepin' there below?)
> Slung atween the round shot, listenin' for the drum,
> An' dreamin' arl the time o' Plymouth Hoe.

An **antimacassar** is put, or by the Victorians was put, over the back of a chair to protect it from the greasy heads of gentlemen who use *Macassar* oil. Macassar is the capital of the island of Celebes in Indonesia, from which the ingredients of this hair-oil were imported in the early nineteenth century. It comes in the White Knight's song in *Alice through the Looking-Glass*:

> His accents mild took up the tale:
> He said 'I go my ways,
> And when I find a mountain-rill,

> I set it in a blaze;
> And thence they make a stuff they call
> Rowland's Macassar-Oil –
> Yet twopence-halfpenny is all
> They give me for my toil.'

Antimacassars have somehow become symbolic of the Victorian age when they were popular. In 1938 the magazine *Scrutiny* referred to 'antimacassar evangelicalism and Sunday-school sanctimoniousness'.

EQUIPMENT, ETC.

These are all artefacts or contraptions for human use:

The **derrick** is called after a Mr *Derrick*. He was a noted professional hangman, who hanged people at Tyburn in the early seventeenth century. He was so enthusiastic about his profession that he constantly strove to improve the equipment, and he finally invented a new sort of specially high gallows, thanks to which the show could be observed from a distance. Later, the word came to be attached to various sorts of gadgets for hoisting heavy weights; a tackle used on board ship, an arm and pulley for raising things to the upper floor of a warehouse, and now the structure over an oil well that supports the drilling machinery.

Another instrument of execution, the **guillotine**, is also called after its inventor, or rather its popularizer. The French physician Dr Joseph Ignace *Guillotin*, elected to the revolutionary constituent assembly, advocated its use partly on humanitarian grounds – it was so quick – and partly to promote revolutionary equality: it was no longer appropriate for the privilege of decapitation to be confined to nobles.

The word has since been used for various sorts of cutting devices; a machine for cutting paper or metal, a surgical contraption for snipping the tonsils. In parliamentary use the guillotine is a method of ending the discussion of a bill by setting a time limit.

jukebox comes from *juke*, 'wicked, disorderly', in the creole language called Gullah spoken by black people of West African descent living on the coast of South Carolina and adjoining islands. A cheap roadhouse or brothel was a juke, and in the 1930s, when technology allowed, they began to be equipped with jukeboxes.

An **umbrella** was originally to keep the sun off you, in climates where that matters, not the rain: Latin *umbra*, 'shade'. They were used in China from the earliest times, seem to have been first noticed in the seventeenth century as something Italians needed, and came into England only a good deal later. (When the dandy Beau Nash, during his regime as master of ceremonies in eighteenth-century Bath, stopped the gentlemen there from carrying swords, he is said to have persuaded them to wield umbrellas instead.)

We certainly think of umbrellas now for keeping us dry, and would probably call the one that keeps the sun off a 'parasol':

> The rain it raineth on the just
> And also on the unjust fella:
> But chiefly on the just, because
> The unjust steals the just's umbrella.

The word is much used figuratively today, as in a *Listener* article of 1965: 'Europe seems unenthusiastic to exchange the American nuclear umbrella for a French one.'

On a similar subject the **mackintosh**, or macintosh, is called after its Glaswegian inventor. Charles *Macintosh* was an early-nineteenth-century chemist whose experiments with tar and naphtha led to the invention and patenting of a waterproof fabric; but now a raincoat is a mackintosh or a mac whatever it is made of.

bangle is a Hindi word. The Hindi *bangri* properly means only a glass one, for the wrist, but a gold one for the ankle still counts as a bangle. Indian wives traditionally break their glass bangles when they become widows.

beads were originally for praying with. The Old English word *gebed* which they come from is related to the modern 'bid'. Each prayer on the rosary was counted by a bead, and a beadsman or beadswoman was a pensioner whose duty was to pray for the soul of the benefactor. The secular use of the word, for the beads in a necklace or strung on an abacus, came a good deal later.

A **cheroot**, the kind of cigar that is open at both ends, gets its name from the Tamil word *shuruttu*, 'a roll'. Cheroots were made

in south India and Manila, and the word was used in English by
the eighteenth century: '60 lbs of Masulipatam cherroots, Rs 500'.

In Kipling's poem 'Mandalay' the British soldier remembers with
longing his Burmese girl:

> I seed her first a-smokin' of a whackin' white cheroot,
> An' a-wastin' Christian kisses on an 'eathen idol's foot . . .

gong is a Malay word, and probably imitates the sound the thing
makes, as when announcing dinner. A familiar domestic object
until quite recently; as a character heartlessly comments in Noël
Coward's *Private Lives* (1930): 'Certain women should be struck
regularly, like gongs.'

It was the shape of this metal disc – exemplified by the big one
that a man strikes at the beginning of J. Arthur Rank's films – that
gave rise to the British slang use of the word to mean a military
medal or civil decoration. Monica Dickens used it like that in *Man
Overboard* (1958): 'Other people came out of the war with Mentions
and worthwhile gongs that tacked letters after their names.'

chopstick is a mixed word, pidgin English in fact; it is not what
the things are called in the countries that chiefly use them. In
pidgin, *chop* or *chop-chop* means 'quick', so chopsticks are 'quick
sticks'. William Dampier explained in his *Voyages and Descriptions*
(1699): 'At their ordinary eating they use two small round sticks
about the length and bigness of a Tobacco-pipe . . . they are called
by the English seamen chopsticks.'

The first sort of **abacus** was apparently a tray of sand for drawing
diagrams in; the Greek word *abakos* comes from the Hebrew *'aḇāḳ*,
'dust'. The square shape of the tray made it natural to use the same
word for the flat slab on top of a column in classical architecture.
But we generally think of an abacus as being a counting frame
within which beads slide on wires.

The system is very ancient. The Romans used the abacus, and
a similar device was known in China as early as the sixth century
BC. They are still common in Eastern countries.

tenterhooks, as when you are 'on tenterhooks' with apprehen-
sion, were the hooks for fastening cloth to a *tenter*. The process

was that webs of cloth were stretched, formerly out of doors, on a wooden framework, and held in place by rows of hooks at the edges. It is from this idea of stretching and straining that we have evolved the modern expression.

The bathroom **geyser** is Icelandic. It comes from *Geysir*, the name of one particular hot spring in Iceland that spouts up like a fountain. There have been geysers, in the bathroom sense, from the 1870s; but they have unfortunately nothing to do with the slang word geezer meaning something like 'chap, fellow'. That comes from *guiser*, 'disguised person, masquerader'.

An **atlas** is called after the giant *Atlas*, who in Greek mythology was punished by Zeus by being made to hold up the pillars of the universe. Homer mentions him in the *Odyssey*: 'The malevolent Atlas, who knows the sea in all its depths and with his own shoulders supports the great columns that hold earth and sky apart'. The pillars were supposed to be approximately at Gibraltar. In the story of Perseus the giant is turned into stone by looking at the Gorgon's head, and becomes the Atlas Mountains in north-west Africa.

The sixteenth-century Flemish geographer Mercator, inventor of Mercator's projection, published a book of maps called *Atlas; or a Geographic Description of the World*. It had as a frontispiece a picture of the giant holding up the world, which is why a map book is an atlas.

The **tumbler** from which one drinks used to *tumble*. The early ones were made with a rounded or pointed base, so that they would not stand upright and had to be emptied at a single draught. They have existed for quite a long time, as Samuel Pepys recorded buying 'two silver tumblers' in his *Diary* for 1664.

The word is also used hard-heartedly in the trade for an inexperienced window-cleaner.

While we are considering dining-room equipment, the **doily** is called after a Mr *Doyley*, a seventeenth-century draper who kept a shop in the Strand. He made a fortune by inventing a cheap, lightweight woollen fabric for summer wear, and that is the first meaning of the word. Dryden referred in 1678 to 'Doily Petticoats'.

The doily as we know it, the frilly lace or paper mat underneath cakes or sandwiches, seems to have been a Victorian invention. That is what the cosy lady is talking about in John Betjeman's poem 'How to Get On in Society' (1954):

> Milk and then just as it comes, dear?
> I'm afraid the preserve's full of stones;
> Beg pardon, I'm soiling the doileys
> With afternoon tea-cakes and scones.

bracket comes, through the Spanish *bragueta*, 'codpiece', from the Latin *bracae*, 'breeches'. How the word came to mean any of the things we now mean by it is one of the mysteries. It has been suggested that the kind of bracket that consists of a right-angle support fastened to a wall, to make a ledge, looks like a pair of breeches. Be that as it may, the English language took account of that sort of bracket by the sixteenth century, and later used the word for a pair of marks to enclose words or figures in writing.

From the idea of enclosing things in typographical brackets comes that of mentioning two or more people or things together to suggest that they have something in common. The statisticians first began to use 'bracket' as a fashionable synonym for 'class' or 'category', which has indeed become something of a cliché in such contexts as 'the upper-income brackets'. This sense has now passed into the general language: by 1956 a character in Michael Innes's *Appleby Plays Chicken* was judging that two men were 'both from the same social bracket'.

Another item of typography. The curious word **ampersand** means the sign &, an adaptation of the written Latin *et*. The word is a corruption of the Latin and English mixed sentence: *and per se – and*, meaning '& by itself = and'. In the old hornbooks from which children learned their letters, the twenty-six letters of the alphabet were followed by the &. A character in George Eliot's *Adam Bede* (1859) thought Z 'had only been put there to finish off th'alphabet like, though ampusand would ha' done as well'.

Some similar printers' abbreviations were once 'a per se, a' which means 'a by itself makes the definite article a'; and 'I per se I', for 'I by itself makes the pronoun I'; and 'O per se' for the interjection

O! They did it to distinguish these words from the mere letters a, i, o.

The **swastika** is another symbol. The ancient Aryan good-luck charm, a cross with each arm continued at a right angle, gets its name from the Sanskrit *svastika*, from *sú*, 'good', + *astí*, 'being'. One sees it carved on temples in India. Hitler adopted the swastika, in its form with clockwise arm continuations, to represent Aryanism in the racialist form in which he used it, meaning non-Semitic; and it survives as a symbol of Fascism and neo-Nazism. It is striking that Kipling used it, entirely because of its Indian associations, on the jackets of his earlier books, but dropped it after the rise of Hitler.

totem is an untranslatable word from Algonquian, a North American Indian language. What those Indians meant by it was an animal, plant, or other object that gave its name to a particular tribe and was that tribe's emblem. One's totem animal was not to be hunted or eaten.

The word has been used to mean a social group with similar background and standards. In John Buchan's *Greenmantle* (1916) Richard Hannay, a British officer in the First World War, takes a fancy to a German engineer: 'Gaudian was clearly a good fellow, a white man and a gentleman. I could have worked with him, for he belonged to my own totem.'

A totem pole is carved and decorated with totem figures, but the word can now mean a departmental hierarchy: a menial employee is 'low on the totem pole'.

bumf is short for *bum-fodder*, lavatory paper. In nineteenth-century schoolboy slang it could just mean paper, so that a 'bumf-hunt' was a paper-chase. It seems to have been the British army that chiefly took to using the word for tiresome bureaucratic documents.

shampoo is Hindi, from *chhāmpo*, 'press'. In oriental use, to shampoo people was to massage them: 'a pleasing wantonnesse,' as was remarked in 1616, 'and much valued in these hot climes'. In 1813, for instance, we read how a Mahratta wife 'first champoes her husband, and fans him to repose; she then champoes his horse'.

It was only in the nineteenth century that the word came to mean what it means today, the stuff with which one washes one's hair, the carpet, or the car.

magnet comes from *Magnesia*, the ancient name of the Turkish city of Manisa, where magnetic iron oxide or loadstone was first found. Richard Eden referred to it rather oddly in a travel book in 1555: 'The Ilande of Magnete that is the Ilande of the lode stone which is vnder or near abowte the northe pole.' (Perhaps he thought that was why the compass needle points north.)

Swift used the idea of the loadstone magnet rather strikingly in *Gulliver's Travels* (1726). The flying island of Laputa was held aloft by an enormous magnet: 'Upon placing the magnet erect, with its attracting end towards the earth, the island descends; but, when the repelling extremity points downwards, the island mounts directly upwards.'

magazine comes from Arabic: *makẓān*, 'a storehouse'. The poet Herbert used it like that in 'A Priest to the Temple' (published 1652): 'The book of books, the storehouse and magazine of life and comfort, the holy Scriptures'. From being any kind of storehouse, warehouse or depot, the word came by the sixteenth century to mean particularly a store for explosives and ammunition; and later the chamber storing a supply of cartridges to be fed automatically into a gun – today also into a camera or slide projector.

The familiar modern use of the word was in fact invented as a metaphor. In 1731 the *Gentleman's Magazine* was founded, with this explanation: 'This Consideration has induced several Gentlemen to treasure up, as in a Magazine, the most remarkable Pieces on the Subjects abovemention'd.' This sense existed in time to be entered in Dr Johnson's *Dictionary* (1755). He wrote, 'Of late this word has signified a miscellaneous pamphlet, from a periodical miscellany named the *Gentleman's Magazine*, by Edward Cave.'

The outline portrait called a **silhouette** is called after Étienne de *Silhouette*, an eighteenth-century French author and politician. Opinions are divided as to whether he actually made silhouettes himself, as a means of taking likenesses at little expense; or whether (more likely) the name was given in ridicule of his cheese-paring economies when he was controller-general. He did indeed make considerable savings in public spending, but went too far in proposing a land-tax on the estates of the nobility, the reduction of their pensions, and the conversion of their table plate into money, so that a 'silhouette' came to mean a figure reduced to its simplest minimum form.

Before the invention of photography, silhouettes were a cheap way of making family portraits.

WEAPONRY, ETC.

pistol comes to us from the Czech *pišt'al*, through French and German, and this word for a small hand-held firearm has been with us since the sixteenth century. Ancient Pistol, the fire-eating poltroon in *King Henry V*, sometimes thinks of himself as a gun:

> Pistol's cock is up,
> And flashing fire will follow.

Oliver Goldsmith complained, 'There is no arguing with [Dr] Johnson: for when his pistol misses fire, he knocks you down with the butt end of it.'

The way one holds a pistol has given rise to the 'pistol-grip' handle design of anything from a saw to a movie camera.

howitzer is another Czech word: *houfnice*, 'catapult', was originally used for a stone-slinging catapult of the kind the Romans knew. This field gun is, as the *Oxford Dictionary* explains, 'adapted for use in a mountainous country', being conveniently light for transport. Howitzers in the modern sense were known by the early eighteenth century, and used in Marlborough's wars. Nelson used them at sea.

The **bayonet** is – probably – called after the town of *Bayonne*, in the south-west of France. The word first meant a sort of short dagger to hang on one's belt or carry in one's pocket, and then by the seventeenth century the more familiar stabbing blade to be attached to the muzzle of a musket or rifle. The bayonet came to be symbolic of military force; in his speech on American taxation (1774) Edmund Burke warned, 'You are obeyed solely from respect to the bayonet.' Napoleon Bonaparte, no less, defined a revolution as 'an opinion backed by bayonets'. But as a Second World War pacifist slogan had it, 'A bayonet is a weapon with a worker at each end.'

'Bayonets' collectively may mean the infantry rank and file.

blunderbuss is Dutch: *dondeebus*, 'thunder gun'. The word got mixed up in English with 'blunder', presumably because of the wild inaccuracy of the firing – a blunderbuss discharged quantities of balls or slugs all over the place, so was at its best only in defending narrow passages.

Blunderbusses died out centuries ago; but Thackeray included one in his *Rose and the Ring* (1854) which is set in the imaginary kingdom of Paflagonia. Its monarch, King Valoroso XXIV, soliloquizes about his youth, when 'with blunderbuss in hand, I brushed away the early morning dew, and shot the partridge, snipe, or antlered deer!'

It is curious that **musket** and **mosquito** come ultimately from the same Latin word: *musca*, 'a fly'. This infantryman's handgun got the name indirectly, being called a musket after an old word for a small sparrowhawk, and the bird of prey in its turn was a *moschetto* in Italian, 'little fly'. The mosquito, also a little fly, got its name through Spanish and Portuguese. Incidentally mosquitoes belong in this military section too, since Mosquito was the name of a Second World War fighter plane.

The word for the gun has been with us in English since the sixteenth century, and exists in other European languages – Dumas's famous sixteenth-century Three Musketeers were, of course, *mousquetaires*. Stanley Holloway's celebrated monologue 'Sam, Sam, pick up tha' musket', happens at the battle of Waterloo.

boomerang comes from an Australian Aboriginal word of New South Wales, first recorded when the penal colony was founded in 1788 as the word for a curved throwing stick, often so designed as to return to the thrower. In 1830 the *Mechanic's Magazine* commented, 'Captain Cook, when at Botany Bay, having seen the boomerang concluded that it was a wooden sword'; and indeed its curved shape does suggest that of a Turkish scimitar.

The figurative meaning is of course much commoner today. A

plan or course of action that boomerangs backfires, recoiling on its originator. The hero of Christopher Fry's *The Lady's Not for Burning* (1949) describes himself as 'driven and scorched/ By boomerang rages and lunacies . . .' A recent refinement, heard in Edinburgh in 1984, is the 'Scottish boomerang', the exile who constantly sings of returning to his homeland but never does. And a 'boomerang kid' is a young adult who leaves the parental home but then has to return for economic or other reasons.

grenade comes from the French *grenate*, and Spanish *granada*, 'pomegranate', but by the sixteenth century it meant an explosive shell for throwing. Originally it was the task of a **grenadier** to throw grenades. Evelyn mentions in his *Diary* (1678) 'a new sort of soldiers call'd Granadiers, who were dextrous in flinging hand granados'. Grenadiers had to be the tallest and strongest men in the regiment.

They often formed a separate company. When Edmund Gibbon recorded in his *Memoirs* (1796) what an advantage his brief military experience had been to him, he mused, 'The discipline and evolutions of a modern battalion gave me a clearer notion of the phalanx and the legion; and the captain of the Hampshire grenadiers (the reader may smile) has not been useless to the historian of the Roman empire.' The name survives today only in the distinguished context of the Grenadier Guards, the first regiment of the British royal household infantry.

The original **torpedo** was a flat-fish, the electric ray. The fish got its name from the Latin *torpedo*, 'numbness'. Sir Thomas Browne wrote in 1646 of how 'Torpedoes deliver their opium at a distance, and stupifie beyond themselves.' Dr Johnson was thinking of this creature in 1743 when he wrote of a certain Dr Birch, apparently a boring writer: 'Tom Birch is as brisk as a bee in conversation; but no sooner does he take a pen in his hand, than it becomes a torpedo to him, and benumbs all his faculties.'

When the underwater missile was invented in the early nineteenth century it was given the same name. Nowadays a torpedo need not be at all fishlike, since they can be launched from the air.

You can 'torpedo' someone's policy or project, making it inoperative; and one American sense of torpedo is of an enormous sandwich in a long bread roll.

While we are on the subject of missiles, one may notice that **missile** itself comes from the Latin verb *mittere*, 'to send'. Some other things and people that are 'sent' somewhere are **missives**, **missions**, and **missionaries**, all from the same Latin root. It seems odd to associate these comparatively harmless matters with the guided missile, the anti-missile missile, and the intercontinental ballistic missile. But are they always so harmless? Poor Mr Jellyby in Dickens's *Bleak House* (1853), fed up with his wife's exertions on behalf of the natives of Borrioboola-Gha, urged his daughter on her marriage, 'Never have a mission, my dear child.' And we owe the following fine confusion to the great Dr Spooner (1844–1930) himself: 'Poor soul, very sad; her late husband, you know, a very sad death – eaten by missionaries – poor soul!'

tank comes either from a Portuguese word *tanque* or from the Indian language Gujarati: opinions are divided. In any case, its oldest meaning seems to be still current in India, America, and Australia, as a reservoir for storing rainwater. Today the word more usually means any storage chamber for gas or liquid, such as an aquarium for fish or the petrol tank in a car. 'Put a tiger in your tank,' urged Esso.

But the interesting bit is how it came to mean an armoured fighting vehicle. This was a matter of security in the First World War, when during the period of research and manufacture they were given the code-name 'tank'. *The Times* reported in 1916, ' "Tanks" is what these new machines are generally called, and the name has the evident official advantage of being quite undescriptive.'

PLACES

These words divide naturally into man-made 'establishments' such as arsenal and factory, and features of the landscape such as bush and jungle. We take the man-made ones first:

arsenal reached us through various Italian, Spanish, French, and Portuguese forms from the Arabic *dār ṣinā'ah*, meaning a factory or workshop. It early came to mean a dockyard, as with the famous one at Venice where they built galleys; later, an armoury where weapons and munitions are manufactured or just stored. It was in this sense that Franklin D. Roosevelt urged his people to be 'the great arsenal of democracy' in 1940. The word can certainly be used, though, in the wider sense of a storehouse or repertory of anything to be used in attack, so that one might speak of a woman's arsenal of cosmetics.

ghetto probably comes from the Italian *getto*, a foundry, since the Jewish quarter in Venice was established in 1516 on the site of a former foundry; but the origins of the word are mysterious. It may come from another Italian word *borghetto*, a borough or village. In any case, after meaning for centuries the Jewish quarter of a city, it now commonly means any quarter of a city populated by a minority group; particularly, but not only, a crowded slum area. We hear not only of Negro ghettos in America and of Catholic ghettos in Northern Ireland, but of smarter areas altogether: John Le Carré refers to 'Elfenau, Berne's diplomatic ghetto'. The implication is always of an enclosed place, designed either to keep people in or – as with the diplomats – to keep people out.

A **factory** was, in earlier times, not a place where things were actually made, but the foreign trading depot of a European merchant company, such as the British East India Company. The man in charge of it was a *factor*, or a *facteur* (French) or *feitor* (Portuguese). A factor may still today be a business agent or (in Scotland) a bailiff or land-agent, but a factory today is only a place where something is 'manufactured'. Confusingly, the Latin verb *facere* from which all these words come means both 'do' and 'make', like *faire* in French, though the distinction is quite a large one in the English mind: we reckon to 'do' actions and 'make' artefacts. This change of meaning from doing to making should be remembered when one is reading about the early 'factories' of the British Empire.

Although a **monastery** now means the house of a community of monks, the word comes from the Greek *monos*, 'alone', like many other words – monarch, monochrome – that share this meaning of 'one'. This is probably because the first Christian monks were in fact solitary hermits, such as St Anthony in the Egyptian desert in the third century.

An **arena** is a sandy place: Latin *arena*, 'sand'. The ancients strewed sand on the floor of an amphitheatre where combats were held, to soak up the blood. One may see the same thing in a Spanish bullring or an old-fashioned butcher's shop. The word thus came to be used for a battlefield or, by extension, for any place of strenuous action. But it is from the shape of the early amphitheatres that the term 'arena stage' has come to be used for a theatre-in-the-round, where the audience surround the central stage.

canteen comes from the Italian *cantina*, 'wine cellar'. Today we think of it chiefly as the place where one eats at one's factory or office, but its first associations are military, the canteen being a licensed shop or tavern selling food and drink to soldiers. This is the sense in Kipling's 'Gunga Din', where in Hell 'it's always double drills and no canteen'. The word also meant a portable container for water, bottles, cooking utensils, or anything else of that kind which might be needed in camp, and that is why a set of knives and forks can nowadays be called a 'canteen of cutlery'.

The Finnish word **sauna** came into English only quite recently; until after the Second World War it still had to be explained as an exotic Finnish institution. Nowadays it is so familiar as to be the natural way to describe steamy heat. In 1976, for instance, *The Times* referred to 'the sauna-like conditions of the Oxford court during the last five weeks'.

bazaar is a Persian word, *bāzār*. It has been with us for a long time in the sense of an open or covered oriental market, with all the exotic connotation of spicy fragrances and haunting musical rhythms. In 1616, for instance, Purchas's *Pilgrimage* (the source of Coleridge's 'Kubla Khan') referred to 'a great Basar or Market of Brazen wares'. It was the Victorians who thought of using the word for a charitable fund-raising sale of ornamental objects, embroidered, knitted, or painted by its officiating ladies; such as the one in aid of the Wimbledon Social Purity League, at which one of P. G. Wodehouse's heroes was constrained to buy 'a tea-cosy, two Teddy bears, a penwiper, a bowl of wax flowers and a fretwork pipe-rack'.

An **asylum** was first a place of refuge: from the Greek *a-*, 'not', + *sulon*, 'right of seizure'. In English the word first meant a sanctuary from which it was sacrilege to remove criminals or debtors. It only much later came to mean a place for the mentally ill. 'The world is becoming like a lunatic asylum run by lunatics,' as Lloyd George grieved in 1933.

But now that such a place is more politely called a mental hospital, 'asylum' is probably more familiarly used in its original sense, as when a state grants 'political asylum' to a refugee from abroad.

compound is two quite different words. The more familiar one, meaning more or less 'mixture, combination', comes from Latin. But the rarer and more interesting one means a fenced enclosure with a house or factory in it, in an Eastern country. This sort of compound comes from the Malay word *kampong*, and such enclosures were called compounds by the early British merchants in the Malay archipelago. They took the word to India, to China, and indeed all over the place. Miners in South Africa may be housed in a compound, or the word may mean a prison camp or an enclosure for strayed animals.

A **shambles** was originally any kind of bench or stool: Latin *scamnum*. The word came to mean a butcher's table for selling meat, then a meat market, and then a slaughterhouse. Later it meant a general scene of bloodshed, as when in 1794, during the Terror, Coleridge wrote that Robespierre had 'made of Lyons one vast human shambles'. Today the word usually means merely a frightful mess or muddle; as when the *Daily Telegraph* commented in 1978: 'Haiti remains a dictatorship, its economy in a shambles.'

terminus comes, rather boringly, from the Latin word for a terminus. The interesting part is that the Romans did actually have a god called Terminus, who was in charge of boundaries and landmarks. They put up statues to him to mark the edges of areas.

The statues were stylized as a human or animal bust ending in a square pillar or pedestal, and became a commonplace of classical architecture. They are more often called 'terms'.

And now some natural features. Several have changed their meaning in curious ways:

A **planet** is a wanderer. The word comes to us ultimately from the Greek verb *planaomai*, 'to wander'. In serious astronomy it means a body, such as the Earth, moving round a star, but that depends on having the modern or Copernican view of the solar system. In earlier thought, and in astrology today, the Earth is not a planet but on the other hand the sun and moon are, since from our point of view they seem to move. In the older Ptolemaic system, accordingly, the seven planets were in order the Moon, Mercury, Venus, the Sun, Mars, Jupiter, and Saturn; Uranus, Neptune, and Pluto had not yet been discovered. They were mounted on concentric spheres with the Moon nearest to us.

In engineering, a subsidiary wheel driven by another is an epicyclic or planetary wheel, and an electron in orbit round its atomic nucleus is a planetary electron.

The **Arctic** gets its name ultimately from *arktos*, the Greek word for a bear. The bear in question is of course Ursa Major, or the Plough, the northern constellation which points to the Pole Star.

By the fourteenth century Chaucer was using the term Arctic Pole ('pool Artik') in the treatise he wrote to teach his little son Lewis to measure the height of celestial bodies with a device called an astrolabe.

jungle comes from the Hindi *jangal*, 'desert, waste'. A legal code of 1776 records how 'Land waste for five years . . . is called Jungle.' This word, the equivalent in India of the Australian, American, or African 'bush', has shifted its meaning somewhat in its passage into English and has also acquired a figurative sense. It is easy to see how a word which originally meant simply waste or uncultivated ground came to describe such land overgrown with thick vegetation. In English now 'jungle' goes beyond that to suggest (perhaps by association with 'tangle') luxuriant tropical forest, impenetrable and savage, with Tarzan probably swinging through its pendulous creepers.

By 1783 Edmund Burke was speaking in Parliament of 'jungles full of wild beasts'. The word came to be used of thickly overgrown land anywhere, so that Macaulay's *History of England* (1849) describes Sedgemoor as 'overhung with rank jungle'. By the mid nineteenth century it was being used figuratively of any wild tangled mass: Carlyle wrote in 1850 of a 'jungle of red tape', Swinburne in 1867 of the 'jungle of argument', and it is also used of any place of ruthless struggle for survival, such as the classroom in the 1950s film *The Blackboard Jungle*. A city may be thought of as an 'asphalt jungle' or 'concrete jungle'.

bush is interesting, not because of its origins – it comes from Old English, like so much of our core vocabulary – but because, like *creek*, it came to have a new meaning outside Britain. Particularly in Australia and Africa the 'bush' is uncultivated land remote from settlement, or even just the countryside as opposed to the town. In Australia it has developed a mythology comparable to that of the American frontier. W. S. Ransom writes in his preface to the Australian *Macquarie Dictionary*, 'Australians think of the word as their own, rich in connotations peculiar to the country and important in many aspects of their culture.' It is a nostalgic word, suggesting rural simplicity, rugged resourcefulness, and loyalty to comrades. A 'bush-ranger' was a sort of outlaw, such as the folk hero Ned Kelly.

From this special sense of bush, the wider world has gained the expression 'bush telegraph', meaning much the same thing as the 'grapevine': the rapid unofficial spreading of information by word of mouth, ahead of the official channels.

creek is another word of more or less indigenous British origin which has strangely changed its meaning in its passage overseas. The Old Norse word *kriki* which it comes from means a 'nook', and that is more or less what the thing is in Britain: a little narrow harbour or inlet on a coast. In America, Australia, and New Zealand, though, a creek is simply a stream or brook. The *Oxford Dictionary* comments:

Probably the name was originally given by the explorers of a river to the various inlets or arms observed to run out of it, and of which only the mouths were seen in passing; when at a later period these 'creeks' were explored, they were often found to be tributaries of great length; but they retained the designation originally given, and 'creek' thus received an application entirely unknown in Great Britain.

Daphne Du Maurier's book title *Frenchman's Creek* concerns a creek in the British sense, a harbour, but we encounter the American sense in Tom Lehrer's sanguinary American ballad:

> One morning in a fit of pique
> She drowned her father in the creek,
> The water tasted bad for a week
> And we had to make do with gin.

A stream in Britain, of course, may also be called a **beck**, as it is in the north of England (Old Norse *bekkr*), or a **burn** in Scotland (Old English *burna*). That is why in *Auld Lang Syne* (1788) Burns wrote,

> We twa hae paidled i' the burn
> From morning sun till dine.

If he and his boyhood friend had been Americans they would have gone wading in the creek.

A dry, waterless **desert** ought strictly speaking to have been 'deserted', since the Latin adjective *desertus* means 'forsaken, abandoned'. Tacitus expressed the idea, meaning a deserted place, in the famous comment, 'They make a desert, and call it peace,' which he puts into the mouth of a British leader urging resistance to the Roman invaders.

A desert in English once meant any uninhabited place. The banished Duke and his friends in *As You Like It* lived in a forest, but young Orlando describes them as living 'in this desert unaccessible,/ Under the shade of melancholy boughs . . .' We still use the word like that when we speak of a desert island, such as Robinson Crusoe's or the imaginary one in 'Desert Island Discs'. Desert islands are remote and uninhabited and usually tropical, but not necessarily at all dry.

The verb 'to desert', as with military deserters and the title of Goldsmith's poem *The Deserted Village*, goes back to the same source; but one's 'deserts' in the sense of behaviour meriting reward or punishment, are quite different, being related to 'deserve'.

WINDS

These words tend to come from the language of the place where that particular wind blows:

The **monsoon**, the seasonal wind of the Indian Ocean, gets its name through Portuguese from the Arabic *mawsim*, 'fixed season'. It appears that the Portuguese picked up the word from the Arab pilots sailing those seas, this dependable wind being of vital importance in the days of sailing ships. It is the south-west monsoon that brings the summer rainy season.

In some sense, 'monsoon' also meant 'season'. In the early days of British trading in India, such was the horrific death rate from infectious disease that it was wryly commented, 'Two Mussoons are the Age of a Man.'

A **typhoon** is a cyclonic storm in the neighbourhood of the China Seas, and accordingly gets its name partly from the Chinese *tai fung*, 'big wind', though also partly from the Arabic *ṭūfān*, 'storm'. The word has existed in English since the sixteenth century, and its spelling in English has been affected by its similarity to *Typhon*, the name of a mythical Greek giant who was the father of the winds. He lies buried under Etna.

tornado is another confused word, a mixture of two Spanish ones: *tronada*, 'thunderstorm', and *tornar*, 'turn'. It is Spanish because the word was first used by navigators of the tropical Atlantic; but now it chiefly means a violent rotatory wind within a small area, such as the funnel-shaped cyclones of the Mississippi region. It was this sort of wind on the Kansas prairie that carried young Dorothy and her dog and the whole house to the land of the Munchkins, in L. Frank Baum's *Wizard of Oz*.

hurricane comes, through Spanish and Portuguese, from *hurakan* in Taino, a former language of the Bahamas and Antilles. It first meant a violent cyclone in the West Indies, which is where the early seafarers heard the word. Robert Parke explained it in 1588: 'This word Vracan, in the Indian tongue of those Ilands, is as much as to say, as the ioyninge of all the foure principall winds togither.' Shakespeare must have liked the sound of it, and used it (1605) in *King Lear*:

> Blow, winds, and crack your cheeks! rage! blow!
> You cataracts and hurricanoes, spout
> Till you have drench'd our steeples, drown'd the cocks!

In precise meteorological terms a hurricane is a wind of force 12, the highest category on the Beaufort Scale.

blizzard was originally an American word. In the American West it meant a sharp blow, or an overwhelming argument, and was so used in 1834 by Colonel Davy Crockett, no less, the Tennessee folk hero: 'A gentleman at dinner asked me for a toast; and supposing he meant to have some fun at my expense, I concluded to go ahead, and give him and his likes a blizzard.'

A blizzard only later came to mean a violent snowstorm with high winds, and in that sense passed into world English. By 1912 the purely British Captain Scott of the Antarctic was using the word in his journal of his ill-fated expedition. When Captain Oates was too ill to travel further, he gallantly gave his life to try to save his companions. 'He said, "I am just going outside, and may be some time." He went out into the blizzard and we have not seen him since.'

SUBSTANCES

This group comprises not 'things' but 'stuff'. First, three elements: the element **cobalt** is the same word as the German *Kobold*, a kind of gnome who lived in mines. Kobolds were apparently nasty little creatures – unlike Snow White's amiable Seven Dwarfs – since the German miners in the Harz mountains gave their name to this ore, both because it was at that time thought worthless and because it was bad for the miners' health.

quicksilver is another name for the metallic element **mercury**. This sense of *quick* means 'alive', as in 'the quick and the dead', and they called it that because of its property of being liquid at ordinary temperatures. It seems to run about as if it were alive.

The Roman god Mercury, corresponding to the Greek Hermes, was the messenger of the gods, lively and volatile – mercurial, in fact – and these qualities were attributed in astrology to the planet that bears his name and in medieval alchemy to the metal. The alchemists attached great importance to this substance. In Chaucer's *Canterbury Tales* (*c.* 1386) the alchemist's assistant explains how each planet has its appropriate metal:

> Sol gold is, and Luna silver we threpe,
> Mars iren, Mercury quyk–silver we clepe . . .

Mercury is used in thermometers, as everyone knows, and has some applications in medicine, though not (as formerly) for syphilis.

Lloyd George complained: 'Negotiating with de Valera . . . is like trying to pick up mercury with a fork.'

copper was *cuprum* in Latin, and its chemical symbol is still Cu. But it comes ultimately from the name of the island of Cyprus, where it was chiefly found in ancient times: *Cyprium aes*, 'Cyprus metal'. Since copper and tin are the ingredients of bronze, copper was a crucially important substance during the Bronze Age.

Cyprus was sacred to Venus, or Aphrodite, who is supposed to have emerged there from the sea. Hence, the alchemists' symbol for copper was the same as that of Venus, ♀, familiar to us today as symbolizing the female, in zoos and elsewhere.

'Copper' coins are no longer made of copper, and probably the old-fashioned domestic copper for boiling the laundry in wasn't copper either. Copper as a slang word for a policeman is nothing to do with the metal – a policeman is someone who 'cops' you.

And now some vegetable products:

rubber in the sense of the latex of the rubber plant is so called because you can rub out pencil marks with it; not the other way round. The word existed, of course, long before the discovery of the rubber plant *Ficus elastica*, to mean various sorts of brushes, towels, or scratchers for rubbing things with, or indeed to mean people who massage you. But when caoutchouc was introduced from South America in the eighteenth century, it was found to rub out pencil much more effectively than the various materials, such as breadcrumbs, that artists and writers had had to use before. (Columbus had noticed the stuff centuries before, when he visited South America, but the main thing that struck him about it was that it *bounced*.)

In American use, 'rubbers' are galoshes, and have been for a long time. In 1852 the poet Emily Dickinson wrote, 'I'll take my india-rubbers in case the wind should blow.' But a 'rubber' has meant a condom only since the Second World War; and 'rubber' in the sense of a match at various games, such as bridge, has nothing to do with any of this, and is a quite different word of mysterious origin. An old word, though. Traditionally, Sir Francis Drake decided to finish his 'rubber' of bowls on Plymouth Hoe before setting out to tackle the advancing Armada.

gum – in the sticky sense – going back through French, Latin, and Greek, comes ultimately from *kemai* in Egyptian, the language used in ancient Egypt until the third century A D. Herodotus, writing in the fifth century B C, describes how it was used in embalming mummies. After various other rather disgusting processes, 'The body is washed and then wrapped from head to foot in linen cut into strips and smeared on the under side with gum, which is commonly used by the Egyptians instead of glue.'

English has had the word since Chaucer's time, in the sense of a secretion from trees and shrubs, and more recently to mean various other gooey substances. The American sense of 'gum' for chewing-gum goes back to quite early in the nineteenth century. President Lyndon Johnson is quoted as saying, 'Jerry Ford is so dumb he can't fart and chew gum at the same time.'

quinine is Peruvian or 'Jesuit's' bark. The word comes from the Spanish spelling of *kina*, 'bark', in Quechua, a language of Peru. This bark of the tropical tree *cinchona* was early found to be useful in reducing fevers, and was brought to Spain by the Jesuits, who knew it from their South American missions. As the bitter flavouring agent in the 'tonic water' which goes into today's gin and tonic, it was formerly important as a prophylactic to ward off malaria. In his *Family Medicine in India* (1873) Sir William Moore advised, 'During unhealthy seasons, or in malarious localities, persons would do well to take a grain or two of quinine daily.' It is still used in the treatment of cramp, and of certain heart conditions.

The tree, by the way, was called after the wife of Chinchon, the Spanish viceroy of Peru. She was cured of a fever by quinine.

belladonna means 'beautiful lady' in Italian. This name for the poisonous plant, deadly nightshade, arose because the plant is a source of the alkaloid drug atropine. Atropine dilates the pupils of the eyes, and a synthetic form is used by eye doctors. But the Italian ladies found that dilated pupils gave them an alluring look of attentiveness. It cannot have been very good for them.

tobacco comes, through the Spanish *tabaco*, probably from Taino, a language of the Antilles and Bahamas. When Columbus arrived there he found the Indians smoking tobacco leaves rolled into a primitive cigar. By the end of the sixteenth century people in England were smoking it, chewing it, or using it in the form of snuff, despite the publication of *A Counterblast to Tobacco* (1604) by King James I himself, no less.

In fact, controversy has raged over the virtues and vices of tobacco ever since its discovery. It was early regarded as a medicine. In Spenser's *Faerie Queene* (1590) the huntress Belphoebe uses it to dress somebody's wound:

> Into the woods thenceforth in hast she went,
> To seeke for hearbes, that mote him remedy ...
> There, whether it diuine *Tobacco* were,
> Or *Panachoea*, or *Polygony*,
>   She found ...

Burton in his *Anatomy of Melancholy* (1621) had mixed feelings about it:

Tobacco, divine, rare, superexcellent tobacco, which goes far beyond all their panaceas, potable gold, and philosopher's stones, a sovereign remedy to all diseases ... But, as it is commonly abused by most men, which take it as tinkers do ale, 'tis a plague, a mischief, a violent purger of goods, lands, health ...

In 1815 Charles Lamb was writing about the agonies of giving up smoking: 'This very night I am going to leave off Tobacco! Surely there must be some other world in which this unconquerable purpose shall be realised.'

The existence of tobacco, though, has been useful in other ways. Sherlock Holmes was assisted in solving the 'Boscombe Valley Mystery' (1891) by the fact that he had written 'a little monograph on the ashes of 140 different varieties of pipe, cigar, and cigarette tobacco'.

indigo comes ultimately from the Greek *indikon*, 'Indian'. This blue dye was first mentioned in English in the sixteenth century, when it began to be imported from the East. (It is a herb rather like woad.) In 1665 Pepys recorded, 'We did agree a bargain of £5000 ... for silk, cinnamon, nutmegs, and indigo.' The production of indigo was an important industry in India. One of the ways in which the discreditable Amory in Thackeray's *Pendennis* (1849) tried to make a living was that he 'set up as an indigo planter and failed'.

Its distinctive colour was listed by Newton as one of the seven primary colours of the rainbow, between blue and violet. In 1843, for instance, Carlyle wrote of 'the sunny plains and deep indigo transparent skies of Italy'.

Now, some miscellaneous substances:

The smelly gas **ammonia** gets its name from the shrine and oracle of Jupiter *Ammon* in a Libyan oasis. It is obtained from sal ammoniac, 'salt of Ammon'. (Ammon is the Greek name of the horned Egyptian god Amun.) This crystalline salt was said to come from the dung of the camels in the desert round the shrine. The priests apparently sent it to Egypt in palm-leaf baskets.

The purple gemstone **amethyst** is supposed to prevent you from getting drunk: Greek *amethustos*, 'not drunk'. It appears that the ancient Greeks sometimes wore amethysts, or made drinking-cups of the stone, to stave off the effects of a drunken party. The superstition was still believed as late as 1596, when Thomas Lodge wrote in *A Margarite of America*, 'The amethist staieth drunkennesse.'

jade is another stone with mystic properties. The name comes from the Spanish *piedra de ijada*, 'stone for the flank, or loins'; i.e. for the renal colic, which it was supposed to cure. Sir Walter Ralegh mentions using bits of jade for 'spleen stones'. It is not too clear how they used it – apparently simply applying it to the painful area was thought to be effective. American Indians used to wear jade amulets against snake bite.

The shiny black mineral **jet** gets its name, through Old French, from the Greek *gagates*, from the town *Gagai* in Asia Minor. (It was called 'gagate' in Old English, but became 'jet' by the fourteenth century.) Jet was popular with the Victorians in the form of mourning jewellery, in an age when mourning was taken very seriously; but it has been used in Britain since prehistoric times, and turns up in Bronze Age round barrows. It was particularly found near

Whitby in Yorkshire, where the local monks used it for their rosary beads.

The word has often been used as the name of a colour. In 1716 Lady Mary Wortley Montagu, the famous bluestocking who introduced smallpox inoculation into Britain, wrote of some women with 'snowy foreheads and bosoms, jet eyebrows'.

turquoise comes through Old French and means *Turkish* (stone). This bluish-green gemstone first came from Persia, and was known here, under various spellings, by the fourteenth century. In *The Merchant of Venice*, Shylock is infuriated to learn that his runaway daughter Jessica has exchanged his favourite ring for a monkey: 'It was my turquoise; I had it of Leah when I was a bachelor: I would not have given it for a wilderness of monkeys.'

porcelain has a roundabout sort of origin. The French *porcelaine* and Italian *porcellana* first meant a cowrie shell, and came from *porca*, 'a sow'. They may have thought the shell was shaped like a sow's vulva. But the hard, glossy surface of the cowrie apparently made Marco Polo apply the Italian word in the thirteenth century to the fine ceramic which he saw for the first time in China. This Chinese porcelain was far more delicate than anything that was to be produced in Europe for centuries. At last, by 1825, Jeremy Bentham was to write, 'The potteries of Wedgwood and Bentley have excelled the porcelain of China.'

And **china** itself, of course, is called after China. Its inhabitants did not call their own country by that name, but the Persian word *chīnī* came to be used in India, and so by the seventeenth century in England, for the delicate and valuable ware first manufactured in China. In Pope's *Rape of the Lock* (1714) the heroine is threatened by some unknown tragedy; but it cannot be predicted

> Whether the nymph shall break Diana's law,
> Or some frail China jar receive a flaw;
> Or stain her honour or her new brocade . . .

Pope later praised his friend Martha Blount as being able to withstand that particular misfortune: 'Mistress of herself, tho' China fall.'

One's 'china' of course may be one's husband, wife, or simply chum. The rhyming slang goes 'mate = china plate'.

manure is really a sort of euphemism. It comes, through the Old French *manuvrer*, from the Latin *manus*, 'hand', + *operari*, 'to work', and is thus closely related to **manoeuvre**. Originally, to 'manure' land was to administer or manage it, then to sow and cultivate it by manual labour, and only later, in the sixteenth century, to put fertilizer on it. By that time the noun 'manure' had come to mean dung or compost. In 1549 we read of a Cambridge college tending its lawn: 'The seyde College dothe . . . laye ther mucke and meanor . . . apon the foreseyde common grene.'

In 1787 Thomas Jefferson used the word unforgettably in a figurative sense: 'The tree of liberty must be refreshed from time to time with the blood of patriots and tyrants. It is its natural manure.'

MONEY

The word **money** itself comes through Old French from the Latin *moneta*, which was a title of the Roman goddess Juno. The ancient Romans minted money in one of her temples on the Capitoline Hill, where she was worshipped as the 'warning' goddess – *moneta* comes from the verb *monere*, 'to warn', as do such English words as 'admonish' and 'monitor', and **mint** goes back to the same root. Money first meant coins, as it did for the king in the nursery rhyme who sat 'in his counting-house, counting out his money', and later meant purchasing power in the wider sense.

Through the ages people have moralized both for and against money. One may choose between St Paul's warning in his Epistle to Timothy: 'The love of money is the root of all evil,' and Dr Johnson's conflicting advice to a friend: 'There are few ways in which a man can be more innocently employed than in getting money.'

bank, in the money sense (or more recently the sense of a blood bank or eye bank) comes through French *banque* or Italian *banca*; the bank of a river through Middle English; and a 'bank' of electrical switches or typewriter keys from Old French; but all are ultimately related to the word *bench*. In the money sense, this would be the table or counter of a money-dealer. So **bankrupt** comes from the Italian *banca rotta*, 'broken bench'. Johnson suggests that when an Italian money-changer became insolvent 'his bench was broke', and one can well imagine it being smashed by enraged depositors. But of course this was no longer literally true in the case of the 'Man who Broke the Bank at Monte Carlo'.

An **exchequer** was first a chessboard; the Old French word *eschequier* comes from the medieval Latin *scaccarium*, and that is what they both meant. It seems that under the Norman kings the accounts of the national revenue were managed by moving counters about on a cloth marked with squares. We must remember how cumbersome bookkeeping must have been before the introduction of Arabic numerals.

cash is a confusing sort of word. In the sixteenth century it meant a money box or till, like the French *caisse*. But another word 'cash', meaning a small copper coin in China or India, goes right back to the Sanskrit *karsha*, and the Europeans trading in the East seem to have mixed them up. The Eastern cash was often the kind with a hole in the middle that can be threaded on a string.

Now cash usually just means money. As Nigel Dennis put it in *Cards of Identity* (1955): 'The moment of reading out the will is one of the few occasions when capital drops its striped trousers and reveals itself as none other than naked cash.'

A **salary**, Latin *salarium*, comes from *sal*, 'salt'. This was the money paid to Roman soldiers to buy salt with; and hence, their pay. It appears that in earlier times they were given an actual salt ration in kind, for which money was later substituted. The word is recorded in English by the fourteenth century, to mean particularly the stipend paid to a priest.

The rather pompous word **emolument** was originally the money paid to a miller for grinding corn: Latin *emolumentum*, from *molere*, 'to grind', which is what one's 'molars' do. This word has been with us since the fifteenth century to mean reward or salary, and for a time it could also mean advantage or benefit. Lord Chesterfield in his *Letters* (1756) describes how he took an emetic, and then 'brought it all up again to my great advantage and emolument'.

loot is the Hindi word *lūṭ*, 'plunder', from the Sanskrit *lotra*. It first came into English as something that particularly happened in India. Colin Campbell wrote to his sister in 1842: 'I have already told you that I did not take any loot – the Indian word for plunder – so that I have nothing of that kind, to which so many in this expedition [the Sikh War] helped themselves so bountifully.'

The word was soon used as a verb. Writing in 1847 of Soult, Wellington's antagonist in the Peninsular War, Lord Malmesbury commented, 'Went to see Marshall Soult's pictures which he looted in Spain. There are many Murillos, all beautiful.'

Finally, three units of currency:

The **dollar** gets its name from *Joachimstal*, 'St Joachim's valley', the name of a silver mine in Bohemia. The German states used the silver dollar or 'thaler' from the sixteenth century, and the word was also used for the Spanish peso or 'piece of eight' which circulated in the Spanish American colonies. In 1782 Jefferson chose the name dollar for the currency of the newly independent United States of America, on the grounds that 'the [Spanish] dollar is a known coin and the most familiar of all to the mind of the people'. Jefferson also chose the symbol $, which may either stand for 'Spanish' or be a modification of the 8 on Spanish pieces of eight.

The dollar is also of course the chief monetary unit of many other countries, including Canada, Australia, and parts of Latin America, Africa, and south-east Asia.

The gold **guinea** was first coined in 1663 for the Company of Royal Adventurers of England trading with Africa. They traded with *Guinea*, the part of West Africa from Sierra Leone to Benin, and the trade involved the exchange of cloths woven in India for African slaves; a Guinea merchant was a slave-dealer. The coin was minted out of gold from Guinea, and had an elephant on it.

There has been no guinea coin since 1813, but the term was used until recently to mean twenty-one old shillings (£1.05) in the context of professional fees and various luxury purchases. To emphasize this idea of luxury, Beecham's pills were advertised as 'worth a guinea a box'.

In American slang, Guinea is a rude word for an Italian or Spanish immigrant. Damon Runyon used it like that in *Guys and Dolls* (1932): 'A bomb such as these Guineas like to chuck at people they do not like, especially Guineas from Chicago.'

A **talent**, from the Greek *talanton*, was in ancient times a weight or, in several nations, a sum of money. The modern use of the word to mean 'aptitude, ability', comes entirely from Jesus's parable of the talents (Matthew xxv), in which two servants who were entrusted with talents made good use of them, while the third simply buried his share; the moral being, 'Unto everyone that hath shall be given, and he shall have abundance: but from him that hath not shall be taken away even that which he hath.'

John F. Kennedy once described a dinner at the White House for Nobel prizewinners as 'probably the greatest concentration of talent and genius in this house except for perhaps those times when Thomas Jefferson ate alone.'

Now the word often means women (more rarely men) regarded from the point of view of sexual promise. In John Fowles's *The French Lieutenant's Woman* (1969) a group of Victorian rakes visit the London red-light district: 'Women dressed as Parisian bargees, in bowlers and trousers, as sailors, as señoritas, as Sicilian peasant girls; as if the entire casts of the countless neighbouring penny-gaffs had poured out into the street. Far duller the customers – the numerically equal male sex, who, stick in hand and "weed" in mouth, eyed the evening's talent.'

TRANSPORT

Here are some ways of moving about the place, first on land and then on water. (We do not include ways of moving through the air, as those words are all still too new to have gained any interesting patina):

coach comes ultimately from *Kocs*, a village in Hungary, though by the sixteenth century the word had passed into most European languages. Coaches, in the sense of a fairly large four-wheeled carriage, were in use in Elizabethan times: poor mad Ophelia cries 'Come, my coach! Good night , ladies . . .' and by 1668 Samuel Pepys wrote proudly of going 'abroad with my wife, the first time that I ever rode in my own coach'.

The size of a hole could be expressed by saying that one might turn a coach and four or a coach and six (horses) in it, or drive them through it. In 1700 someone called Sir Stephen Rice is recorded as claiming that he would 'drive a coach and six through the Act of Settlement [of Protestants in Ireland]'.

When the roads were improved and coaches had proper springs, it became a popular hobby for dashing young gentlemen to drive a coach and four. The dexterity and stamina required by this sport led to the use of the word coach for a private tutor or athletic trainer.

Later, of course, 'coach' came to mean a railway carriage; and, still later, a single-decker bus.

juggernaut is a title, *Jagannath*, of the Hindu god Vishnu, and means 'lord of the world'. His image was dragged in procession through the streets of Puri in Orissa, on an enormous chariot, sometimes crushing people under the wheels. (There may be no foundation for the popular belief that devotees threw themselves under it on purpose.) That is how the idea developed of a force that crushes everything in its path; so that when the unhappy statesman Huskisson was run over by Stephenson's 'Rocket' on the opening of the Liverpool to Manchester railway in 1830, they said at the time that he had been Juggernauted. Today we apply the word to a large heavy lorry, particularly an articulated one, when we think of it as noisy or dangerous.

bus is short for the Latin *omnibus*, which means 'for everybody'. The full form of the word was first used in Paris for a public vehicle plying for hire along a fixed route, and then adopted by one Shillibeer when he started a bus service – horse-drawn, of course – from Paddington to the City. The plurals of these words are correctly buses and omnibuses, despite the misguided efforts of people who know a little Latin and think it ought to be bi and omnibi. In 1914 A. D. Godley wrote a joke poem about that:

> What is this that roareth thus?
> Can it be a Motor Bus?
> Yes, the smell and hideous hum
> Indicat Motorem Bum . . .

An omnibus, of course (though not a bus) can also be a one-volume collection of novels or stories that were previously published separately.

tandem is, like omnibus, another word taken straight from Latin, but this one is a sort of pun. *Tandem* in Latin means 'at length', in the sense of 'at last, finally'. That is what it meant in the motto on the banners of Bonny Prince Charlie, the Young Pretender of the 1745 Jacobite Rebellion: *Tandem Triumphans* (At last triumphant). As a joke, a vehicle pulled by two horses harnessed one in front of the other was described, from the eighteenth century onwards, as a tandem, because of the way the horses were arranged. When the bicycle was invented the same word was used for the kind where one cyclist sits in front of the other. (Apparently this arrangement is difficult for the one at the back, who has to pedal without being able to steer.)

caravan comes from the Persian *kārwān*, and first meant a group of travellers, perhaps merchants or pilgrims, banded together to cross a desert or a stretch of dangerous territory. One may imagine something like the wagon train by which the early settlers penetrated the American West, though the early caravans of Asia were usually a procession not of vehicles but of laden camels. When caravan means a house on wheels, one to be towed by a car or horse, like Toad's 'gipsy caravan, shining with newness, painted a canary-yellow picked out with green, and red wheels' in *The Wind in the Willows*, or else a 'camper' with its own motive power, it is often abbreviated to **van**, the word we always use for the familiar covered goods vehicle on the road, or for part of a British railway train.

cab is short for the French *cabriolet*, which meant a sort of light chaise pulled by one horse. The vehicle got its name because it went so terrifyingly fast that it reminded people of a leaping goat. (The Latin *caper*, from which the word comes, means a goat, and gives us the verb to **caper**.)

Cabriolets were introduced into London in the early nineteenth century. The word was soon shortened to cab, which has come to mean the modern taxi.

'Get me a cab,' said the American writer Robert Benchley as he stepped out of a night club. The uniformed figure at the door protested angrily that he was not a doorman but a rear admiral. 'OK,' said Benchley, 'get me a battleship.'

rickshaw. As a general policy this book discusses only words for things, people, or places that actually exist in English-speaking countries. We break that rule here; first, because there really are rickshaws in India, and other Asian countries, where English is the main second language; secondly, because of the curious etymology; and thirdly because of an interesting change of meaning. The word is abbreviated from the Japanese *jinrikisha*: *jin*, 'person', + *riki*, 'power', + *sha*, 'vehicle'. The thing, originally a two-wheeled vehicle pulled by a man, has largely given way in Eastern cities today to the cycle-rickshaw, a sort of tricycle pedalled by one man in front with seats for two people at the back, and – even more modern – the auto-rickshaw, a sort of little taxi with a motorbike engine that seats two people behind the driver: this last being no longer 'person-powered' at all.

And here are some ways of travelling on snow:

sleigh and **sledge** both come to us from the Dutch *slee* and *sleedse*, but **toboggan** is from Algonquian, an American Indian language. Apparently sleigh is the preferred American and Canadian word for the large vehicle pulled by horses, dogs, or reindeer. That is what is going on in the rousing ditty

> Jingle, bells! jingle, bells! jingle all the way,
> Oh! what fun it is to ride in a one-horse open sleigh.

They tend to call the small downhill one a **sled** (Middle Low German *sledde*), while the British might say sledge for both. In Marlowe's *Tamburlaine* (1586), though, the hero promises the lady he is wooing:

> With milk-white harts upon an ivory sled
> Thou shalt be drawn amidst the frozen pools,
> And scale the icy mountains' lofty tops . . .

ski is a Norwegian word; and in its language of origin is pronounced like 'she'. Now that skiing has become a world sport, the change of pronunciation may owe something to the fact that the original way of saying it is rather rude in French: *chier* means 'shit'.

And here are a few boats:

canoe comes through Spanish from Arawakan, a language family of South America and the West Indies. Columbus found the word in use when he reached the New World, and it reached English in about 1560. Originally it meant a boat that is sharp at both ends and is propelled by paddles, not oars. It was applied to light frame boats covered with stretched skins, like the coracle or Eskimo kayak, or with birchbark like the North American Indian ones, or to the primitive 'dugout' canoe. (The modern French *canot* is not the same word. It simply means a small boat or a dinghy, though the word is used in French-speaking Canada for Canadian canoes.)

The phrase 'paddle one's own canoe' seems to have been originated by the rather manly Captain Frederick Marryat, author of *Mr Midshipman Easy* and of several Victorian boys' books.

A Canadian has been defined as 'somebody who knows how to make love in a canoe'.

dinghy comes from the Bengali and Hindi *ḍĩṅgī*, 'a little boat'. From being part of the vocabulary of British India, it came to be the official term for a small extra boat on a naval or merchant ship. Today of course it may well be motorized, and may also be an inflatable rubber one.

Also from the Indian subcontinent comes **catamaran**, but this time from Tamil, a language of south India: *kaṭṭumaram*, 'tied wood'. This kind of boat with twin hulls was used in the coastal waters of south India, and the word came to be used for the same thing in the West Indies and off South America. In the Napoleonic wars a catamaran was a kind of explosive fireship, a forerunner of the torpedo, prepared in order to resist Napoleon's invasion of England. It may have been this meaning, perhaps influenced by the word 'cat', that gave rise to the colloquial sense of catamaran as a shrewish quarrelsome woman.

coracle and **currach** are the Welsh and Irish words, respectively, for the ancient kind of boat constructed by draping watertight material (originally animal hides, more recently tarred canvas) over a framework. They have been used for many centuries for fishing, transport, and even dipping sheep; the small ones on lakes and rivers, bigger ones on the sea. It was presumably in a currach that St Columba crossed the Irish Sea in 563, from Ireland to the island of Iona, to convert the Picts.

Another kind of framework boat is the **kayak**, this time an Eskimo word. In those Arctic waters the boat was traditionally covered with sealskin, and the man kept himself dry by lacing himself into a skin covering. The word is now used for any slim, covered canoe developed from the Eskimo version.

yacht is the Dutch *jaghte*. A *jaghtschip* was a fast pirate ship, and the first part means 'chase, hunt'. Though no longer piratical, we still think of a yacht as something light and fast. Since the British had trouble with this Dutch word, its spellings have been, as the *Oxford English Dictionary* says, 'various and erratic', but the word has been with us for a long time: Evelyn reports in his *Diary* (1661), 'I sailed this morning with his Majesty in one of his Yatchts (or pleasure boats), vessels not known among us till the Dutch East India Company presented that curious piece to the King.' There seems never to have been too much trouble over how to pronounce it, though, as may be observed from the rhyme in Edward Lear's poem (1877):

> Does he teach his subjects to roast and bake?
> Does he sail about on an inland lake,
>
> > in a YACHT
> > The Akond of Swat?

OCCUPATIONS AND EVENTS

The first three 'occupations' are decidedly to do with horses. A **steeplechase** was originally exactly what the name suggests: from the late eighteenth century onwards a group of riders, often on their way back from a day's hunting, would choose a distant church steeple as a landmark. They raced for it across the then much more open country, jumping any hedges and ditches on the way. The modern steeplechase, such as the Grand National at Aintree, or a similar event on foot, simulates this early idea but over a prepared course.

The game **polo** has a much more exotic origin. Its name comes from Balti, a language of Tibet, where it means 'ball'. British cavalry officers in India took up this expensive, dangerous, and exciting game of hockey on horseback and brought it to England by the 1870s, and from there it spread to the rest of the world. Cheaper variants are water polo, played by swimmers, and similar games played on roller skates or on ice.

A **gymkhana** today suggests a set of competitive games for little girls on ponies. The word comes, though, from the Hindi *gendkhāna*, 'ball-house', the name given to a racket-court, and then to a public place in Anglo-India with sports facilities. It then got mixed up with the word *gym*. Even now in India a Gymkhana Club may have a swimming-pool, cricket pitch, and tennis courts, but probably has nothing to do with horses.

To move from land to water, a **regatta** (not surprisingly) origin-ates in Venice, where it was the word for boat races between gondoliers on the Grand Canal. It means 'contest'. The Venetians were holding regattas by the seventeenth century, and one first took place on the Thames in 1775, when Dr Johnson wrote to his friend Mrs Thrale about it: 'I am glad that you are to be at the regatta.'

A **cruise**, however, is of Dutch origin: *kruisen* means 'cross, traverse', but the word has for a long time meant 'sail to and fro'. By the mid seventeenth century one reads of the Dutch admiral Van Trump 'with his fleete crusinge about Silly', and 'cruise' has since been used of ships cruising in pursuit of other ships, or of whales, or simply for pleasure. Johnson defines it as 'to rove over the sea in search of opportunities to plunder; to wander on the sea without any certain course'.

Now, some miscellaneous occupations:

barbecue comes, through Spanish, from the Haitian word *barbaca*, which first meant a raised wooden framework for sleeping on or for smoking and drying meat, and was used in that sense in English by the seventeenth century. Then it came to mean the familiar iron framework for outdoor cooking, meat cooked that way, or a party for eating it. Johnson recorded the word, illustrating it by a quotation from one of Pope's 'Satires' about a famous glutton:

> Oldfield with more than Harpy throat endued,
> Cries 'Send me, Gods! a whole Hog barbecued!'

What Pope meant by this, apparently, was 'a hog roasted whole, stuffed with spice, and basted with Madeira wine'. Delicious but filling.

Barbecuing is so popular in Australia that they have shortened it to 'barby'.

The festivities of the **carnival**, celebrated in Catholic countries before Lent, come rather surprisingly from the Latin *carnem levare*, 'removal of meat', i.e. before the Lenten fast. The word was known in English from the sixteenth century as the name of an Italian festival. In 1646 the diarist Evelyn wrote of 'Shrovetide, when all the worlde repair to Venice, to see the folly and madnesse of the Carnevalle'. Nowadays 'carnival' may mean any festival, especially one involving a fancy-dress procession, and in America it means a travelling funfair.

To strike a more cultural note, **opera** comes from the Italian and thence from Latin, where it means 'work, labour'. The Italians invented the opera, and the diarists Evelyn and Pepys both attended them in the seventeenth century. Evelyn recorded in 1645 how he went to one in Venice: 'This night . . . we went to the Opera where comedies and other plays are represented in recitative musiq . . . with variety of sceanes painted . . . and machines for flying in the aire . . . one of the most magnificent and expensive diversions the wit of man can invent.'

The opera has indeed always had some connotation of the high-falutin. Edith Wharton commented in 1920, 'An unalterable and unquestioned law of the musical world required that the German text of French operas sung by Swedish artists should be translated into Italian for the clearer understanding of English-speaking audiences.' And W. H. Auden wrote in 1967, 'No opera plot can be sensible, for in sensible situations people do not sing. An opera plot must be, in both senses of the word, a melodrama.'

Nowadays, more prosaically, a 'horse opera' is a Western film and a 'soap opera' is of course a sentimental TV serial of domestic life – the first ones having been sponsored by soap companies.

safari is from the Arabic *safar*, 'journey', and reached us through Swahili, but only fairly recently; in 1928 the *Daily Express* still felt it had to explain the word: 'the royal safari – as a shooting expedition of this nature is described in Africa . . .' In these 'greener' or more humanitarian days, when so many wild animals belong to protected species, a safari is more often undertaken for photography or simply for tourism, but the word has certainly become popular. There are safari boots, safari jackets, and, in this country, safari parks where one can watch the lions from the safety of one's own car.

The appalling Hindu rite of **suttee**, the burning of a widow on her husband's funeral pyre, is very ancient, and the word for it goes back to Sanskrit: *satī*, 'faithful wife'. (It originally meant the woman, rather than the act of suicide.) This Indian custom was noted by the ancient Greeks, and by Marco Polo. It was declared illegal in British India in 1829, but took a long time to stamp out, being connected with the Hindu belief in transmigration – the woman's burning herself would secure immortal bliss for both wife and husband.

Another Hindu custom, **yoga**, is also ancient enough to have been noted by Marco Polo in the thirteenth century: 'There is another class of people called Chughi who . . . form a religious order devoted to the Idols.' The word comes from the Sanskrit *yoga*, 'union', with which is ultimately connected our more familiar term **yoke**. Originally a system of meditation and asceticism, yoga is more familiar in the West today for the physical exercises and breath control associated with it. Aldous Huxley became interested in yoga in the 1930s, and now there seem to be yoga classes and yoga instructors in every suburb.

ABSTRACTIONS

Not 'things', these, but 'concepts'. First come some to do with words and language:

pidgin is the way Chinese traders pronounced the word *business* when they were negotiating with Europeans at Chinese seaports. 'Pidgin English' was thus 'business English', used for communication between these two peoples who had no common language. A rudimentary pidgin may arise wherever people of different language groups are thrown together, but it may go on being useful within a country, as in multilingual Papua New Guinea, where Melanesian pidgin is the language of administration.

Pidgin (or pigeon) means business too in the phrase 'That's your pidgin.' John Wyndham used it in *The Midwich Cuckoos* (1957): ' "Not our kind of job," he said, with the air of one recalling a useful Union decision. "More like the fire chaps' pigeon, I'd say." '

patter, in the sense of a conjuror's or street trader's rapid speech or the 'patter songs' in the Gilbert and Sullivan operas, is short for *Paternoster*. It seems that that was the way people used to say their prayers, in a sort of rapid mutter. The moss-trooper William of Deloraine in Scott's *Lay of the Last Minstrel* (1805) apologizes:

> Prayer know I hardly one;
> For mass or prayer can I rarely tarry,
> Save to patter an Ave Mary,
> When I ride on a Border foray.

In the traditional Order for Morning Prayer in the Church of England prayerbook, the priest is enjoined to 'say the Lord's Prayer with an audible voice', presumably rather than 'pattering' it.

W. S. Gilbert used the word in *Ruddigore* (1887) in a patter song, to be sung very fast:

> This particularly rapid, unintelligible patter
> Isn't generally heard, and if it is it doesn't matter.

hocus-pocus was the stage name of a certain seventeenth-century conjuror. Apparently it was the beginning of a nonsense formula which he used to rattle off, like a spell, to distract the attention of the audience before doing a trick: 'Hocus pocus, tontus talontus, vade celeriter jubeo.' This was thought to be a corruption of the Latin *Hoc est corpus*, 'This is the body', which the priest intones at the moment of transubstantiation in the Mass; implying, blasphemously, that the changing of the bread and wine into the body and blood of Christ is another conjuring trick.

From hocus-pocus comes the verb **hocus**, and probably also **hoax**. One can hocus (= hoax) a person, or hocus (= drug) a drink. Dickens used the verb that way in *Pickwick Papers* (1837). At the Eatanswill election, Sam Weller recounts how

the opposite party bribed the bar-maid at the Town Arms, to hocus the brandy and water of fourteen unpolled electors as was a stoppin' in the house.

'What do you mean by "hocussing" brandy and water?' enquired Mr Pickwick.

'Puttin' laud'num in it,' replied Sam.

An **anthology** was once a collection of flowers: Greek *anthos*, 'flower', + *-logia*, 'collection'. The *Greek Anthology* was a collection of 'flowers of verse', short poems by various authors. There is in fact an obsolete sense of 'anthology' to mean a book about flowers, in the same way that zoology is about animals and ornithology is about birds.

grammar and **glamour** sound the same when pronounced by a Japanese speaker who has trouble distinguishing r from l; but few of us would realize that they really are the same word. In the Middle Ages the Latin *grammatica* meant the study of Latin – that was what 'grammar schools' were originally for – and this was taken to imply scholarship in general, the studies of the learned classes. These studies would include magic and the occult sciences. Thus the word 'glamour', a corruption of 'grammar', grew up with the meaning of an enchantment or spell. To 'cast the glamour over' someone was to deceive their eyes by enchantment. Sir Walter Scott explained the term in his *Letters on Demonology and Witchcraft* (1830): 'This species of Witchcraft is well known in Scotland as the glamour, or *deception visus*, and was supposed to be a special attribute of the race of Gipsies.'

Hence 'glamour' came to mean a magical beauty, and the word was enthusiastically taken up from the thirties onwards, particularly in America and particularly in the contexts of advertising and showbiz. It now meant chiefly physical allure, which is about where we stand with it today. The pundit Eric Partridge in the 1940s was still abusing it as a nasty new coinage: 'A girl or a gigolo may possess *glamour*: and it makes no matter whether the girl is glamorous in her own right or by the catch-guinea arts of her dressmaker or her cinematographic producer. *Glamour* has para-trooped its way over . . . current journalism.'

slogan is Gaelic. The Scottish Highland war-cry, the first meaning of this word, was called a *sluagh*, 'army', + *gairm*, 'shout'. This sort of slogan would be the name of a chief, or of a rallying-place. Scott uses it like that when he describes a battle in *The Lay of the Last Minstrel* (1805):

> To heaven the Border slogan rung,
> 'St Mary for the young Buccleuch!'
> The English war-cry answer'd wide . . .

Today slogans belong to either politics or advertising. In 1971, for instance, Sir Harold MacMillan referred to 'the somewhat disingenuous slogan of "ban the bomb"'.

propaganda is Latin. In 1622 a committee of cardinals was founded to oversee foreign missions, with the title of *Congregatio de propaganda fide*, 'congregation for propagating the faith'. Nowadays propaganda is usually a rather discreditable term for the selected information and doctrines publicized by one's adversary. James

Thurber debunked the word nicely in *Fables for Our Time* (1940), with a story about 'a very proper gander' who was accused of fraternizing with hawks and driven out of the country.

An **alibi** comes from the Latin adverb *alibi*, 'elsewhere', and the word was once used in English as an adverb. An eighteenth-century writer on legal matters mentions a prisoner who 'endeavoured to prove himself alibi'. Then it came to be a noun, as it is today, meaning a plea that one must be innocent of a crime because one was somewhere else. T. S. Eliot used it correctly in *Old Possum's Book of Practical Cats* (1939):

> Macavity, Macavity, there's no one like Macavity,
> There never was a Cat of such deceitfulness and suavity.
> He always has an alibi, and one or two to spare:
> At whatever time the deed took place – Macavity wasn't there!

In this century the word has often been used to mean any kind of pretext or excuse; and you can now alibi someone, which makes it a verb.

sarcasm comes from the Greek *sarkazō*, 'tear flesh, gnash teeth'. (One may recognize the Greek *sark*, 'flesh', which crops up in various medical words and in sarcophagus.) So when we use bitter, sarcastic language we are metaphorically biting someone. A nasty idea really. As Thomas Carlyle remarked in *Sartor Resartus* (1833), 'Sarcasm I now see to be, in general, the language of the devil.'

bosh is Turkish. The Turkish adjective *boş* means 'empty, worthless'. This colloquial word came into English in 1834, in James Morier's then popular novel of oriental life, *Ayesha*. Kingsley was using it by 1863 in *The Water Babies*. His Professor Ptthmllnsprts delivered a paper at the British Association asserting that 'nymphs, satyrs, fauns . . . imps, bogies, or worse, were nothing at all, and pure bosh and wind'.

bunkum was first spelt 'buncombe', and comes from the name of *Buncombe* County in North Carolina. In the course of a debate in Congress, the member for that district insisted on addressing the house in flowery and impassioned terms, although everyone begged him to shut up. He said that his consistuency expected it, and that he was bound to 'make a speech to Buncombe'. In American political contexts, such phrases as 'speak to buncombe' or 'make a bid for buncombe' thus came to mean any political claptrap undertaken to please the electors. This useful word was taken up in British writing to mean any kind of empty oratory or humbug.

Not surprisingly, **bunk** in the sense of nonsense is short for bunkum; as when Henry Ford told a reporter in 1916 that 'History is more or less bunk.'

And now some words about numbers and measurements:

average, curiously, comes from the Arabic *'awār*, 'damage or loss at sea'. The word was first used in connection with the sea trade of the Mediterranean. It meant the expense to the owner caused by damage at sea to a ship or to its cargo. In maritime law, such expense was equally distributed, where necessary, among several interested parties according to the proportion of their involvement, and was defined in the seventeenth century as 'a certaine contribution that merchants and others doe every man proportionably make toward their losses, who have their goods cast into the sea for the safegard of the shippe, or of the goods and lives of them in the shippe in time of a tempest'. It thus came to mean the distribution of inequalities among the members of a set, and the equalizing so achieved. That is how we reach the modern non-mathematical use to mean 'the ordinary standard', as when Bing Crosby asked for his epitaph to read 'He was an average guy who could carry a tune.'

digit comes from the Latin *digitus*, 'finger'. It can still mean a finger, thumb, or toe, and is correctly used like that in contexts of zoology or comparative anatomy. But the Romans used the breadth of a finger as a unit of measurement equal to an inch or ¾ of an inch, a subdivision of the foot. (These measurements are all based on the normal human body. A **cubit** – Latin *cubitum*, 'elbow' – was the distance from elbow to fingertip, and we still measure horses by the hand and spirits by the finger.)

Since people instinctively count on their fingers, a digit came to be any of the numerals below ten – or sometimes including 0 – which can be expressed in the Arabic system by a single figure.

Astronomers still use the word to mean a measurement rather than a number. In their sense, a digit is a twelfth of the diameter of the sun or moon, and is used in expressing the extent of an eclipse.

digital can also be used in the 'finger' sense: creatures with toes, such as cats, are digital-footed, but horses are not. But today, of course, we think of this word chiefly in the context of digital watches, with digits instead of hands, and digital electronic processes in the computer world, which represent data as a series of digits.

A **furlong** was originally a *furrow-long*. In the open-field system of medieval agriculture, each peasant cultivator would plough several strips in the common field, running right across a square containing about ten acres. This rather vague ancient measure was later standardized as 220 yards, an eighth of a mile.

When a **brace** means two, as with a pair of hounds, it probably comes from the use of the word to mean a strap with which the creatures were coupled together. The Old French word *brace* means the width of a pair of outstretched arms, and it gave rise also to 'brace' meaning one of the brackets { and } used in printing words and music, as well as to various other sorts of braces such as the kind that hold up trousers.

The musical **breve** originally meant a 'short' note, being a variant of *brief*; which is odd, since this very long note scarcely occurs in modern music. But when in the Middle Ages people first tried to record precise musical time values, there were two notes longer than the breve. These longer ones have both fallen into disuse, and shorter ones have been devised – which does not, of course, mean that music is now played faster.

In the medieval system the **minim**, from the Latin *minimus*, 'smallest,' was what its name implies.

calibre is originally an Arabic word: *ḳālib*, 'a mould for casting metal'. This came to mean first the diameter of a bullet or cannonball and then the internal bore of the gun that fired it. In the sixteenth century the word was already used with reference to the early guns called harquebuses. Only later did it come to apply to the diameter of anything cylindrical, such as a column or an artery; but it was quite soon used of a person's degree of ability or merit, as when one tries to find an employee of sufficient calibre for an important post.

Curiously, **calliper** is the same word, since one used 'calliper compasses' to measure the calibre of shot or the internal dimensions of a gun. The shape of this contraption, with a pair of curved legs, led to the use of the same word for the kind of splint that supports a leg.

tariff comes ultimately from the Arabic *ta'rīf(a)*, 'notification'. In English it first meant an official list of customs duties, and later on any table of fixed charges, such as that of a hotel. In 1751 Viscount Bolingbroke used the word sardonically: 'The church of Rome found it necessary to publish a tariff, or book of rates, which I have seen in print, wherein the price is set over against every sin, lest purchasers should be imposed upon.'

The lovely word **googol** was invented, in 1940, by a little boy of nine called Milton Sirotta, who was asked to think of a good name for a very large number. It means 'ten to the power of a hundred', or 1 followed by 100 zeros. This splendid child went on to recommend the name **googolplex** for an even larger number, ten to the power of a googol.

algebra comes from the Arabic *al*, 'the', + *jabr*, 'reunion'. Its oldest sense in English, which came to us from the Moors in Spain, was thus the surgical setting of broken bones. The Arabs also used the word in the meaning that we know today, for the science that represents numbers and quantities by symbols. The connection seems to be that an algebraic equation is a sort of 'reunion'.

While we are on these mathematical matters, **algorithm** (or algorism) celebrates the name of the ninth-century Arab mathematician *al-Kuwārizmī*. Through the translation of his work in the twelfth century, Arabic numerals first reached Europe. The word first meant Arabic or decimal notation, and hence arithmetic. It has only quite recently come to mean a set of rules, as used in computer programming or machine translation.

Arabic notation, in contrast with the Roman system, depends on the existence of the **zero**, 'o'. It reached us through French or Italian, but is ultimately the Arabic *ṣifr*. We have come to use the word in all sorts of technical contexts, not only in arithmetic but in such situations as the freezing-point of water on thermometers, in phrases such as 'zero population growth', and in America for pronouncing telephone numbers.

Now some assorted misfortunes:

A **disaster** happens when the stars are against you. The Italian *disastro* comes from *astrum*, the Latin for star or planet. An unfavourable arrangement of the heavenly bodies was a presage of calamity. In *Hamlet*, Horatio recounts how the stars foretold the murder of Julius Caesar:

> A little ere the mighty Julius fell,
> The graves stood tenantless, and the sheeted dead
> Did squeak and gibber in the Roman streets:
> As stars with trains of fire and dews of blood,
> Disasters in the sun . . .

The condition of **delirium** is that of a plough that gets out of line and ploughs a crooked furrow: Latin *delirare*, from *lira*, 'a ridge'. A close parallel would be the modern slang expression 'off one's trolley'.

Milton invented **pandemonium**. His Pandaemonium, in *Paradise Lost* (1667), was the great capital and council chamber of all the devils in Hell: the Greek *pan*, 'all', + *daimon*, 'devil':

> Built like a Temple, where Pilasters round
> Were set, and Doric pillars overlaid
> With Golden Architrave . . .

Satan summons there 'A solemn Councel forthwith to be held/ At Pandaemonium' to discuss what steps should be taken to restore the fallen fortunes of all the devils driven out of heaven.

So far, Pandemonium sounds an orderly sort of place, though of course infernal. It only later came to be thought of as a scene of violent uproar and confusion. By 1865 Francis Parkman, in his *Pioneers of France in the New World*, could write that 'When night came, it brought with it a pandemonium of dancing and whooping, drumming and feasting.'

smithereens ('smashed into smithereens') is probably the Irish *smidirin*, but has been with us in English only since the 1820s. The Irish diminutive *-een* makes the fragments that something has been smashed into sound even smaller! James Joyce (who was after all Irish) used it (1922) in *Ulysses*: 'Crew and cargo in smithereens.'

anathema is Greek. It first meant 'a thing devoted, an offering to the gods', but later came to mean 'an accursed thing'. It was also used for the church's formal curse of excommunication. Gladstone wrote in 1844: 'The Pope ... has condemned the slave trade – but no more heed is paid to his anathema than to the passing wind.'

This word is now more often used for something that a person hates; so that one might say, 'The use of nuclear power is anathema to him.'

Most of the many senses of the common word **check** come from its use in chess, which is Persian. The Persian *šāh*, 'king', is what one says when a move exposes the opponent's king. If there is no escape for the king, the game ends with **checkmate**, which is *šāh māt*, 'the king is dead'. These chess words have existed in English since at least the fourteenth century. In his *Book of the Duchess* (1369), mourning the early death of John of Gaunt's wife, Chaucer describes a losing game of chess played against Fortune:

> There with Fortune seyde, 'Checke here,
> And mate in the mid point of the checkere.'

forlorn hope is a mistranslation from the Dutch: a *verloren hoop* is a 'lost troop', which originally meant an advance party of picked skirmishers, or a storming party, sent on ahead of an attacking army. The Duke of Wellington used the phrase (1799) in this correct meaning, in a dispatch: 'The forlorn hope of each attack consisted of a sergeant and twelve Europeans.'

But it was very early misunderstood to mean a faint remaining chance of success; the connection presumably being the idea that, as Johnson explains in his *Dictionary*, the forlorn hope were 'the soldiers who are sent on first to attack, and are therefore doomed to perish'.

short shrift is ecclesiastical in origin. The shrift part of it means confession to a priest, with the consequent penance and absolution. 'Have you got leave to go to shrift today?' inquires the Nurse in *Romeo and Juliet*. A criminal who was condemned to execution was allowed just enough time to make his confession quickly. Shakespeare uses the expression like that in *King Richard III*, when Sir Richard Ratcliff feels that the condemned Lord Hastings is delaying matters by talking too much:

> Dispatch, my lord; the duke would be at dinner:
> Make a short shrift; he longs to see your head.

Now the expression just means 'curt, unsympathetic treatment'.

And now four words about the senses:

instinct, the innate impulse to behave in a particular way, comes from the Latin *in-*, 'towards', + *stinguere*, 'prick'. The word could once mean simply a natural tendency: one eighteenth-century writer on architecture, for instance, referred to 'a natural instinct in all heavy bodies to lean and press upon the lowest parts'. But it came to be used only of the impulses of living creatures, in the way Gibbon used it in his *Decline and Fall of the Roman Empire* (1781): 'The operation of instinct is more sure and simple than that of reason: it is much easier to ascertain the appetites of a quadruped, than the speculations of a philosopher.'

The colloquial British **shufti**, meaning 'look, glimpse', is from the Arabic *šaffa*, 'try to see', and seems to have been with us since the Second World War. About 1943 people began to say, 'Take a shufti at this.' Accordingly a shufti-kite was a reconnaissance aircraft, and a shufti-scope a telescope or periscope: an expression used more recently for the device with which Customs officers search the cavities of a vehicle for smuggled contraband.

A **butcher's**, meaning a look, is British rhyming slang with the rhyming word left out: *butcher's* hook: 'Have a butcher's at this.' But the Australians and New Zealanders use the word differently and base it on a different rhyme: in their version, to 'go crook' is to lose one's temper, and to 'go butcher's' means that too. Hook rhymes there with crook, not with look, it seems.

When a **raspberry** is a rude noise made with one's lips, it is another bit of rhyming slang, with the rhyme word as so often omitted: *raspberry* tart = fart. This expression has been around since the late nineteenth century, long enough to have developed the figurative sense of a refusal or reprimand; as in a *Punch* article of 1927: 'I have embodied the above suggestions in a memo, and they are now on their way to the Army Council . . . They may even be on their way back, with a raspberry from Somebody Very Senior written across the top left-hand corner.'

To finish the subject of 'abstractions': a **pedigree** is a 'crane's foot', from the Old French *pie de grue*. When a genealogical table is drawn out on paper, the branching lines of descent look like a bird's claws. This word has existed in English under various spellings since the Middle Ages. For instance, the poet John Lydgate referred in 1426 to 'a peedeugre how that . . . Henry the sext, is truly borne heir unto the corone of Fraunce'. We now use it, of course, with reference to the descent of pure-bred animals, but it can also mean the 'provenance' of a work of art, or a person's criminal record, or indeed the traceable origin of anything.

serendipity means the faculty of making happy discoveries by accident. *Serendip* was an old name for Sri Lanka. In 1754 Sir Horace Walpole wrote to tell his friend Horace Mann of this new word he had just invented, which he defined as 'accidental sagacity':

I once read a silly fairy tale, called 'The Three Princes of Serendip': as their Highnesses travelled, they were always making discoveries, by accidents and sagacity, of things which they were not in quest of: for instance, one of them discovered that a mule blind of the right eye had travelled the same road lately, because the grass was eaten only on the left side . . .

Walpole's word has become popular in this century, in such contexts as the accidental discoveries of science. Columbus's discovery of America when he expected to reach the Indies has been described as 'the greatest serendipity of history'.

It is hard to see why an **indenture** should have anything to do with teeth; but it has. The Latin *dens, dentis*, 'tooth', as in 'dentist', forms part of the verb **indent**, which can mean to make jagged notches in something. The first legal sense of 'indenture' was of a covenant between two parties drawn up in duplicate on one piece of paper, and then cut in two with a jagged line, so that when the two parts were put together they would exactly fit, showing that they were parts of the same document, and that as Johnson's *Dictionary* has it, 'any want of conformity may discover a fraud'.

backlog was originally an American word for the big log that is put at the back of a log fire and will go on smouldering, perhaps for days. In 1782 St J. de Crèvecoeur wrote of winter on an American farm: 'The careful Negro, Jack, who has been busily employed in carrying wood to the shed that he may not be at a loss to kindle fire in the morning, comes into his master's room carrying on his hip an enormous back-log without which a fire is supposed to be imperfectly made and to be devoid of heat.'

The Americans have had the word in that sense since the seventeenth century. It has only more recently come to mean an accumulated reserve; or arrears of uncompleted work, unprocessed materials, unfulfilled orders.

taboo, or tabu, comes from the Polynesian language of Tonga in the south-west Pacific. Captain Cook first heard the word there in 1777 during his voyages, and his subsequent account of the matter brought the word into English: 'When any thing is forbidden to be eat, or made use of, they say, that it is *taboo*.' In its original Polynesian sense, 'taboo' was chiefly applied to things that were too sacred for general use, but now it usually means that something (such as a dirty word) is prohibited by social custom.

NOT NOUNS

We end with a collection of interesting adjectives and verbs. Some polite adjectives first:

sturdy is mysteriously connected with thrushes. This adjective, which today means robust and vigorous, has come up in the world. The Old French word *esturdi*, 'dazed', comes from the Latin *ex* + *turdus*, 'thrush', since thrushes were believed to get drunk from eating overripe grapes. There is a disease of sheep called sturdy, which makes them giddy, and the related adjective came to mean impetuously violent in war, then stern and obstinate, then stalwart and perhaps uncompromising. Sturdy beggars and vagabonds were the able-bodied and perhaps violent ones, considered undeserving of charity.

auspicious also involves birds. In ancient Rome the *auspex* had the task of divining the auspices, omens of the future, from the flight of birds or by examining their entrails: *avis*, 'bird' (as in 'aviary'), + *spex*, 'observer' (like 'spectator'). Favourable omens were auspicious, so the word came to mean 'favourable'; as when at the end of *The Tempest* Prospero promises the King of Naples

> calm seas, auspicious gales,
> And sail so expeditious, that shall catch
> Your royal fleet far off.

frank, in the sense of 'candid, undisguised, open', comes from the Latin *francus*, 'free'. When Gaul was conquered in the sixth century, only the conquering Germanic Franks, as the dominant people, were free rather than being slaves or serfs.

The 'franking' of a letter with a franking machine, instead of using an ordinary stamp, refers to this same meaning of 'free'; and **franchise**, the right to vote, goes back to the same origin.

posh unfortunately does *not* come, as legend has it, from 'Port Out, Starboard Home', the cooler north-facing cabins on a ship plying between England and India. This beguiling theory seems to have been around since the 1930s, but is quite without foundation. It is more likely that posh comes from an old slang word for a dandy; perhaps deliberately used as a name in George and Weedon Grossmith's *Diary of a Nobody* (1892): 'Mr Posh was worth thousands. "Posh's one-price hat" was a household word in Birmingham, Manchester, Liverpool, and all the big towns throughout England.'

Posh is also used as a verb and an adverb. As a sluttish landlady remarks in Dorothy L. Sayers's *Have His Carcase* (1932): 'I don't get time to posh myself up of a morning.' And in Michael Innes's *The Open House* (1972), John Appleby is afraid that 'a crowd of electricians might well take him for a cunning crook talking posh'.

If something is **colossal**, it is because it resembles a *colossus*, the Greek word for a gigantic statue. The Greek historian Herodotus called the enormous statues of ancient Egypt colossi, but the most famous one in antiquity was the gigantic statue of Apollo beside the harbour at Rhodes. It stood 105 feet high and was one of the seven wonders of the world. (People thought, inaccurately, that it actually stood astride the harbour mouth, which is why Shakespeare made Cassius complain, in *Julius Caesar*, that Caesar

> doth bestride the narrow world
> Like a Colossus, and we petty men
> Walk under his huge legs . .).

More recently, we have come to use colossal to mean more or less 'splendid, magnificent'.

jumbo may or may not come from Mumbo Jumbo, a supposed African bogy or deity:

> Mumbo-Jumbo, God of the Congo
> And all of the other

> Gods of the Congo,
> Mumbo-Jumbo will hoo-doo you

wrote the American poet Vachel Lindsay.

But the word existed in English as early as 1823 to mean a big, clumsy creature or thing. Jumbo was thus the appropriate name of an enormous elephant exhibited in the London Zoo and then sold to Barnum's circus in the US in the late nineteenth century, and it was from him that the word became popular and has come to be used of a large airliner, or indeed of anything very large of its kind, such as a jumbo steak. The name was reputedly given to the elephant by the then superintendent of the London Zoo, a Mr Bartlett.

A **dexterous** person, literally, should use his or her right hand: the Latin *dexter* means 'right'. By contrast, if you are **sinister** you must be using your left: Latin *sinister*, 'left'. (Both dexter and sinister are technical terms in heraldry, where the 'bend sinister' is the sign of bastardy.)

All of this is hard on those of us who, though reasonably skilful and not in the least malignant, are nevertheless left-handed.

happy comes from *hap*, an old word for 'chance, luck, destiny'. One may recognize the same idea in *haply*, meaning 'perhaps': 'Haply the Queen-Moon is on her throne,' as Keats wrote in his 'Ode to a Nightingale' (1819).

But 'happy' very early came to mean, not 'accidental' but 'lucky'. When Robinson Crusoe found Friday's footprint in the sand, he concluded that his island had been visited by savages, and 'was very thankful in my thoughts that I was so happy as not to be thereabouts at that time'.

The chief modern meaning of the word, something like 'cheerful and contented', arose only rather later. That is presumably what it means in the American Declaration of Independence (1776), which asserts the human right to 'life, liberty, and the pursuit of happiness'.

cushy came into English only in this century, from the Hindi *khūsh*, 'pleasant'. It seems to have been first used in the Indian army, and then to have passed into general military use in the First World War: a soldiers' word. A 'cushy' wound in that war was one that was not serious. In Evelyn Waugh's *Decline and Fall* (1928) the egregious Captain Grimes escapes a court martial to be 'sent to Ireland on a pretty cushy job connected with postal service'.

The word often carried a slightly disapproving suggestion that one was being let down too lightly – perhaps because of its likeness to 'cushiony'. In Siegfried Sassoon's *Memoirs of an Infantry Officer* (1930) he comments: 'There were times when I felt perversely indignant at the "cushiness" of my convalescent existence.'

The word **agnostic** was invented at a party in Clapham in 1869, by the great biologist Professor Thomas Huxley. He derived it from the Greek *a*, 'not', + *gnostos*, 'knowable'. He had in mind the episode in the seventeenth chapter of Acts, in which St Paul preaching in Athens draws the attention of his listeners to an altar dedicated to 'The Unknown God'. The word describes the mental attitude of those who neither accept nor reject what is incapable of proof.

adamant is usually nowadays an adjective meaning 'stubborn, inflexible'. In Nevil Shute's *No Highway* (1948) a little Farnborough boffin makes himself such a nuisance – justifiably, as it turns out – on a plane at Gander that the airline 'were adamant that they would not carry Mr Honey back across the Atlantic on one of their aircraft'. But, originally, adamant was a noun. The Greek word is *a*, 'not', + *damao*, 'to tame'. It meant anything very hard, such as steel. In *Paradise Lost* (1667) Milton describes the fall of Lucifer from Heaven:

> Him the Almighty Power
> Hurl'd headlong flaming from the ethereal sky,
> With hideous ruin and combustion, down
> To bottomless perdition; there to dwell
> In adamantine chains and penal fire . . .

Adamant also came to mean magnetic iron oxide, or loadstone.

*

And now some less flattering adjectives:

The Latin adjective *horridus*, from which comes the English **horrid**, could mean 'bristling, shaggy', which horrid has been used for in English. In Burton's *Anatomy of Melancholy* (1621) someone had a 'horrid beard'. It came to mean 'rough, wild, savage', and was much used in that sense when describing scenery; in his *Voyages* (1772) Captain Cook commented: 'Nothing in nature can make a more horrid appearance than the rugged mountains that form Table Bay.'

Things that are rough, savage, etc., frighten us, and that is the sense in which little Catherine Morland in Jane Austen's *Northanger Abbey* (1818) gloats over the offer of some Gothic horror novels of the school of Mrs Radcliffe's *Mysteries of Udolpho*: 'Are they all horrid? Are you sure they are all horrid?'

Gradually the sense became weakened, so that today something horrid is less likely to be terrifying and revolting than merely nasty and disagreeable; as with the little girl in the rhyme, who

> When she was good
> She was very, very good,
> But when she was bad she was horrid.

Dr Johnson says that this last sense of the word is 'women's cant', and the *Oxford Dictionary* apparently agrees: 'Especially frequent as a feminine term of strong aversion'.

naughty comes from *naught*, 'nothing', and the oldest sense of the adjective was 'having nothing', in fact 'needy'. Langland in *Piers Plowman* (1377) urges his readers to be charitable to people who are naughty.

The word came to mean 'wicked', and then later to be applied to disobedient children – as in Enid Blyton's title *The Naughtiest Girl in the School*. More recently, it often means 'sexually indecent', as with the Naughty Nineties of the last century. One's sexual organs are thus the 'naughty bits'.

bizarre comes through French, Spanish, and Portuguese, but ultimately from Basque, the language spoken round the Bay of Biscay, which apparently has no connection with any other language in the world. The Basque word *bizarra* means 'beard'. Since bizarre now means something like 'eccentric and grotesque', it is hard to see the connection with beardedness; but apparently in older French the word meant 'brave and soldier-like', from which one must suppose that proper soldiers had beards. They did in *As You Like It*, being 'full of strange oaths, and bearded like the pard'.

puny is a spelling of the older *puisne*, an Old French word meaning 'later born' (*puis* + *ne*) and hence 'junior and subordinate'. In legal use, a puisne judge is one inferior in rank to the chief justices. The Anglicized spelling came to be used of a novice or tyro, or of anything weak and tiny.

maudlin is a corruption of *Magdalen(e)*; which is in fact pronounced like that as the names of two colleges at Oxford and Cambridge:

> The men of Magdalene
> They must have been dagdalene . . .

Mary Magdalene, or Mary of Magdala, out of whom Jesus cast seven devils, has traditionally been identified with the unnamed repentant prostitute of Luke vii, who 'stood at [Jesus'] feet behind him weeping, and began to wash his feet with tears, and did wipe them with the hairs of her head'. She was elevated into sainthood and is portrayed as a weeping penitent: 'drawn by painters', as Johnson has it, 'with swoln eyes, and disordered look, a drunken countenance . . .' From her representation in art comes the meaning of the adjective as 'mawkishly sentimental and effusive', particularly as a symptom of drunkenness.

tawdry comes from another female saint. According to Bede's *Ecclesiastical History of the English People* (731) St Audrey, or Etheldrida, died of a tumour of the throat. This she accepted as a just retribution for having in her youth adorned her neck with splendid necklaces. She was the patron saint of Ely, and cheap silk neckties called 'tawdry laces' were sold there at St Audrey's Fair. In *The Winter's Tale* the shepherdess Mopsa coaxes her sweetheart to buy one from the pedlar: 'Come, you promised me a tawdry-lace and a pair of sweet gloves.' The adjective came to be used of cheap, shoddy finery in general.

If something is **preposterous**, it is out of its natural order: Latin *prae*, 'before', + *posterus*, 'coming after'; as when one puts the cart before the horse. It soon came to mean 'perverse, contrary to nature and common sense'. Johnson in his *Dictionary* quotes Bacon in illustration: 'Put a case of a land of Amazons, where the whole government, publick and private, is in the hands of women: is not such a *preposterous* government against the first order of nature, for women to rule men, and in itself void?'

Usually now preposterous means simply 'absurd', as it did when John Gay remarked in 1713, 'The muff and fur are preposterous in June.'

trivial, 'trifling and unimportant', comes from the Latin *trivialis*, 'commonplace'. This in its turn comes from *tri*, 'three', + *via*, 'road'. The ideas of three-ness and of triviality are united in the name of the Trivium, the elementary course at a medieval university which dealt with the three subjects of grammar, rhetoric, and logic. This course was naturally less prestigious (more 'trivial') than the Quadrivium to which an advanced student would proceed, which embraced the *four* subjects of astronomy, music, geometry, and arithmetic. These seven subjects together constituted the Seven Liberal Arts.

In biology, the trivial name of a plant or animal is that which distinguishes its particular species within the wider genus; or else its common vernacular name as opposed to its technical one.

Anything **antediluvian** existed before Noah's Flood: Latin *ante*, 'before', + *diluvium*, 'flood'. Various writers of the seventeenth and eighteenth centuries used it that way. They refer particularly to the reputed long life span of 'antediluvian' people such as Methu-selah in the Book of Genesis. The elderly wooer Sir Sampson, in Congreve's *Love for Love* (1695) boasts of his undiminished vigour: 'I am of your patriarchs, I, a branch of one of your antediluvian families, fellows that the flood could not wash away.' But the word now usually means very primitive and antiquated.

If something is **grotesque**, it belongs in a grotto. The Italian word *grottesca* was defined, in 1611, as 'antick or landskip worke of Painters'. The idea is that the Romans of that period used the word 'grottoes' for the subterranean rooms of classical Rome that were beginning to be discovered by excavation, and when they imitated the antique murals that they saw there they were painting the kind of thing you might find in a grotto: pictures of people and creatures fantastically distorted and intertwined with flowers and foliage. One may see the kind of thing at Pompeii.

In his *Religio Medici* (1643) Sir Thomas Browne used the word when he was discussing the evidences of God's wisdom in designing all living creatures: 'There are no Grotesques in Nature; not anything framed to fill up empty Cantons, and unnecessary spaces.' And Milton used it in *Paradise Lost* (1667) to describe a ruggedly romantic landscape. His Garden of Eden is placed high on the top of

> a steep wilderness, whose hairy sides
> With thicket overgrown, grotesque and wild,
> Access denied.

Nowadays the word usually means something like 'monstrous and absurd'. Sherlock Holmes, confronted with a case of Voodooism that entailed the sacrifice of a white cock and a black goat, commented drily: 'There is but one step from the grotesque to the horrible.'

Anything **dilapidated** was once, literally, demolished by scattering its stones: Latin *di*, 'asunder', + *lapidare*, 'throw stones'. The word was thus first used of buildings, as when Sir Thomas Herbert referred in 1634 to 'a ruined Chappell ... delapidated by the Dutch'. But it has long been quite properly used of anything fallen into disrepair. In 1874 that impeccable stylist Ruskin mentioned 'a large and dilapidated pair of woman's shoes'.

The original sense of the word has to some extent survived in the use of 'dilapidations' for the repairs that an outgoing tenant or clergyman has to pay for on renouncing a tenancy or vicarage. In Jane Austen's *Mansfield Park* (1814) the Revd Mr Norris died, and was succeeded at the Parsonage by Dr Grant, so the widowed Mrs Norris had to pay: 'Dr Grant and Mrs Norris were seldom good friends; their acquaintance had begun in dilapidations . . .'

People who are **lackadaisical** are presumably in the habit of exclaiming '*Alack-a-day!*' This archaic expression of dismay meant something like 'Woe to the day'. It was what Juliet's nurse and Lady Capulet both said when they failed to wake the girl up for her wedding: 'She's dead, deceased, she's dead; alack the day!' But people who said it too often were thought to be feebly sentimental and affected.

Nowadays the word more usually means listless and lazy. It is not clear why the meaning has changed.

The adverb **galore** is Irish, or Scottish, Gaelic: *go léor* means 'enough, plenty'. The word has certainly existed in English since the seventeenth century, though perhaps more often used by Scottish and Irish writers. In 1826, for instance, Sir Walter Scott wrote in his journal that he had 'sent off proofs and copy galore before breakfast'. But when they filmed Sir Compton Mackenzie's comedy *Whisky Galore* (1947), it had to be retitled *Tight Little Island* for the American market; so perhaps 'galore' is not widely known outside Britain.

amok, or amuck, is a Malay word. The *Oxford Dictionary* defines it as 'rushing in a state of frenzy to the commission of indiscriminate murder'. In his *Voyages* (1790) Captain Cook explained, 'To run amock is to get drunk with opium . . . to sally forth from the house, kill the person or persons supposed to have injured the Amock, and any other person that attempts to impede his passage.'

Pope, 'the Wicked Wasp of Twickenham', used the expression figuratively:

> Satire's my weapon, but I'm too discreet
> To run amuck and tilt at all I meet.

If you do something on your **tod**, meaning 'on your own', you are commemorating *Tod* Sloan by means of rhyming slang, which, as so often, has dropped the rhyming word: alone = Tod Sloan = Tod. Tod Sloan was one of a group of American jockeys who emigrated to England in the late nineteenth century, and are said to have revolutionized British racing.

Anything **hermetically** sealed is related in an odd way to *Hermes Trismegistus*, 'thrice-greatest Hermes'. The medieval alchemists gave that name to the Egyptian god Thoth, whom they regarded as the founder of their mystic art. It was they who invented the method of rendering a tube or vessel absolutely airtight by soldering or welding, or by melting the glass to twist and fuse it at the neck.

The term survived the advent of modern science. Thus in 1664 the Irish scientist Robert Boyle (discoverer of Boyle's Law about the relation between the pressure of gas and its volume) wrote a 'Discourse, containing some new Observations about the De-ficiencies of Weather-Glasses, together with some Considerations touching the New or Hermetical Thermometers'.

And now some curious verbs:

To **manufacture** something was originally to make it by hand: Latin *manu*, 'by hand', + *facere*, 'to make'. Bacon used the word like that in *The Advancement of Learning* (1605): 'It is not set down that God said, Let there be heaven and earth . . . but actually, that God made heaven and earth . . . the one carrying the style of a manufacture, and the other of a . . . decree.' The word came later to mean the production of goods on an industrial scale, in a factory and usually with division of labour. It can also mean 'fabricate fictitiously'; as when Edward Gibbon wrote (1762), 'The speech is evidently manufactured by the historian.'

If you **calculate**, or come to that if you use a calculator or employ the integral or differential calculus, you are involved with the Latin word *calculus*. This means a small stone such as might be used in board games like draughts, or in counting on an abacus. A 'calculus' in the medical sense still means a stone: a mineral lump inside the body.

It has been an American regionalism, since at least early in the last century, to use 'calculate' to mean 'think, believe', as in 'I calculate it's going to rain.'

Originally one would **gossip** with a *godsib*, a person who has become a *sib* – a 'relation', as in 'sibling' – through baptism: that is, a godparent or a fellow godparent or one of one's children's godparents. The 'godparent' sense lingered on as a regionalism into the nineteenth century. In *The Daisy Chain* (1856) Charlotte Yonge has a labourer in the quarry promise: 'The children shall be ready, and little Jack too, and I'll find gossips, and let 'em be christened on Sunday.'

The relationship was taken seriously. In Chaucer's *Canterbury Tales* (*c.* 1386) the Parson warns against a kind of incest: 'Right so as he that engendreth a child is his flesshly fader, right so is his godfader his fader espiritueel; for which a wooman may in no lasse synne assemblen with her godsib than with hire owene flesshly brother.'

But one's 'gossips' soon began to mean simply one's close friends, especially a woman's friends and especially those invited to be present at a birth. Then a gossip was any tattling newsmonger, as in Johnson's definition of 'One who runs about tattling like women at a lying-in'. By extension the word came to mean the tattle itself, as it does in Auden's film script *Night Mail* (1936):

> Letters of thanks, letters from banks,
> Letters of joy from girl and boy,
> Receipted bills and invitations
> To inspect new stock or to visit relations,
> And applications for situations,
> And timid lovers' declarations,
> And gossip, gossip from all the nations.

The associated verb goes back to at least Shakespeare's time.

To **orient** or **orientate** something was originally to make it face east, to the *Orient*. Churches are traditionally built, or oriented, with the altar at the east end, and people may be buried with their feet pointing east, apparently so as to be facing the right way at the Resurrection. In ancient times, churches were oriented so that the rising sun would shine upon the altar on their saint's day.

More recently, the word has come to mean finding out where one is with a compass, getting one's bearings; which is what people do in the sport of orienteering.

To **rankle** used to mean literally to fester, in the case of a wound. It goes back to the medieval Latin *dranculus*, 'little dragon, or serpent'. It is not clear whether a festering sore looks like a serpent, or feels like being bitten by one.

Nowadays it is abstract injuries and disappointments that rankle.

When you **procrastinate**, you put something off till tomorrow: the Latin *procrastinare* comes from *pro*, 'forward', and *cras*, 'tomorrow'. In Shaw's *Back to Methuselah*, Adam doesn't feel like weeding the garden today, so he asks the serpent: 'Make me a beautiful word for doing things tomorrow; for that surely is a great and blessed invention.' The serpent replies 'Procrastination'. But as archy comments in Don Marquis's *archy and mehitabel* (1927):

> procrastination is the
> art of keeping
> up with yesterday.

commandeer is from South African Dutch, Afrikaans: *kommanderen*. This word came into use in the 1880s with reference to the actions of the Boers. It meant either forcing people into military service or seizing things for military use. It soon came to mean any sort of arbitrary grabbing; a euphemism for pinch or pilfer, since it makes them sound almost official.

barrack is two verbs with almost opposite meanings and both of Australian origin. One of them means 'shout encouragement' for a team or party. The other and more familiar verb means 'jeer derisively' at opponents in a game. The first may have reached Australia from the Northern Irish word *barrack*, 'to boast of one's fighting powers', and the second is probably from the Australian Aboriginal word *barak*, 'negative'.

The hostile 'barrack' was first used in Australia in a sporting context in the 1880s, and reached English sporting journalism by about the turn of the century. In 1963 *The Times* reported: 'When Miss Truman led 4−1 in the first set, the crowd began to barrack

every point she scored and to encourage the Italian girl with pro-
longed cheering.'

Since barrackers are known to interrupt speeches as well as
games, the word is now used in political contexts. Barracking there
is much the same as heckling, though perhaps not quite so nasty.

escape comes through French from the medieval Latin *ex*,
'out', + *cappa*, 'cloak'. The idea seems to be that the fleeing
prisoner wriggles out of his enveloping garment and runs for it,
leaving the empty cape or coat in the hands of the jailer. The
wriggling is pretty well what an **escapologist** does, someone
like Houdini.

scoff, when it means 'gobble' rather than 'mock', comes through
Afrikaans from Dutch. The Dutch word *schoft* means 'quarter of a
day', and consequently 'meal'. (Did they have four meals a day?)
A somewhat colloquial word, but it has been with us since early
in the nineteenth century. Herman Melville was using it in 1850:
'Some of you fellows keep scoffing as if I had nothing to do . . .
but look on.'

When we **arrive** somewhere, it used to mean that we
reached the land. The word comes ultimately from the Latin *ad*,
'to', + *ripa*, 'shore', and was for a long time used chiefly in the context of ships and seaports. Chaucer wrote of Ulysses 'arriving' at
Circe's isle. As late as the eighteenth century Dr Johnson felt
that this aquatic sense was the proper one, and quoted Dryden in
illustration:

> At length *arriving* on the banks of Nile,
> Wearied with length of ways, and worn with toil,
> She laid her down.

But since the Middle Ages, to arrive somewhere is simply to
get there, physically or figuratively; people can arrive, for instance,
at years of discretion. Robert Louis Stevenson's dictum, 'To travel
hopefully is a better thing than to arrive,' uses the word in the
familiar modern sense.

To **canter** is to ride at the gentle *Canterbury* pace preferred by
medieval pilgrims, such as those in Chaucer, on their way to the

shrine of Thomas à Becket at Canterbury. In 1673 the poet Andrew Marvell referred to prelates 'canterburying from Synod . . . to Synod'. The word was shortened by the eighteenth century. In 1706 it was claimed of a horse advertised in the *London Gazette* that it 'Trots, Paces, and Canters very fine'.

The Italian physiologist Luigi *Galvani* was the first person to **galvanize** anything, and he did it to dead frogs. In 1786 he described his experiments on the action of electricity upon their leg muscles, making them twitch. Today the word usually has nothing to do with electricity, being used either for the coating of iron buckets and suchlike with molten zinc, against rust, or with the figurative meaning 'rouse into action'. Charlotte Brontë used it like that in *Villette* (1853), in the scene where the child Polly plays with the schoolboy Graham Bretton: 'Her approach always galvanized him to new and spasmodic life; the game of romps was sure to be exacted.'

And the Austrian physician Friedrich Mesmer was the first to **mesmerize** people: to hypnotize them by a power first known as 'animal magnetism', which he believed to come from the astrological influence of the planets. He held seances in Vienna, and in 1778 moved to Paris, where the government appointed a commission of the Academy of Sciences to investigate his claims. He was unsuccessful in his attempt to mesmerize one of the members, who happened to be Benjamin Franklin.

The word is now used only figuratively, to mean spellbind or fascinate.

When we **pander** to someone, or to their weaknesses, we imitate the behaviour of the fictional *Pandarus*, the uncle of Cressida or Criseyde in Boccaccio's, Chaucer's, and Shakespeare's versions of the Troilus and Cressida story. Pandarus was the archetypal pimp or procurer, who brought the two lovers together. Shakespeare's Pandarus said: 'Let all pitiful goers-between be called to the world's end after my name; call them all Pandars.'

Nowadays we probably use the verb more than the noun; as does an Edwardian dowager in Alan Bennet's play *Forty Years On* (1968) when she first hears of the Boer war; 'I have never understood this liking for war. It panders to instincts already catered for within the scope of any respectable domestic establishment.'

To **astonish** or **astound** someone once meant to 'stun' them; it may come from the Latin *extonare*, which meant something like 'strike with a thunderbolt'. A sixteenth-century medical treatise mentions 'astonished or benummed parts of the body', and a slightly later one speaks of 'astonishment of the Leg by compression of the Nerves'.

The rather weaker modern meaning came later; as when Clive in 1773 protested against the accusation of having enriched himself excessively in India: 'By God, Mr Chairman, at this moment I stand astonished at my own moderation!' or when the great impresario Diaghilev encouraged Jean Cocteau (though in French, actually) with the immortal words 'Astonish me!'

And finally, the unique **OK**, or okay, which can be an interjection: ' "Pass the jam." "OK" '; or an adverb: 'She can sing OK'; or an adjective: 'The beer's OK'; or a noun: 'He gave it his OK'; or a verb: 'Can you OK these figures?'

It arose in America as early as 1839, apparently as a jocular spelling of the initial letters of 'all correct' when spelt 'orl korrect'. (According to some authorities, that was the way the then President Andrew Jackson used to spell it.) In any case, the abbreviation was adopted as a joke in Boston and New York.

Then in the following year the Democrats took it up as the election slogan of 'Old Kinderhook', the nickname of one Martin Van Buren, who was born at Kinderhook in New York State and ran for the Presidency in 1840. There was at that time a Democratic 'OK Club' in New York City.

A variant coined by astronauts and space engineers is 'AOK', which means 'All Systems Working'.

INDEX

READ MORE IN PENGUIN

In every corner of the world, on every subject under the sun, Penguin represents quality and variety – the very best in publishing today.

For complete information about books available from Penguin – including Puffins, Penguin Classics and Arkana – and how to order them, write to us at the appropriate address below. Please note that for copyright reasons the selection of books varies from country to country.

In the United Kingdom: Please write to *Dept. EP, Penguin Books Ltd, Bath Road, Harmondsworth, West Drayton, Middlesex UB7 ODA*

In the United States: Please write to *Consumer Sales, Penguin USA, P.O. Box 999, Dept. 17109, Bergenfield, New Jersey 07621-0120.* VISA and MasterCard holders call 1-800-253-6476 to order Penguin titles

In Canada: Please write to *Penguin Books Canada Ltd, 10 Alcorn Avenue, Suite 300, Toronto, Ontario M4V 3B2*

In Australia: Please write to *Penguin Books Australia Ltd, P.O. Box 257, Ringwood, Victoria 3134*

In New Zealand: Please write to *Penguin Books (NZ) Ltd, Private Bag 102902, North Shore Mail Centre, Auckland 10*

In India: Please write to *Penguin Books India Pvt Ltd, 706 Eros Apartments, 56 Nehru Place, New Delhi 110 019*

In the Netherlands: Please write to *Penguin Books Netherlands bv, Postbus 3507, NL-1001 AH Amsterdam*

In Germany: Please write to *Penguin Books Deutschland GmbH, Metzlerstrasse 26, 60594 Frankfurt am Main*

In Spain: Please write to *Penguin Books S. A., Bravo Murillo 19, 1° B, 28015 Madrid*

In Italy: Please write to *Penguin Italia s.r.l., Via Felice Casati 20, 1–20124 Milano*

In France: Please write to *Penguin France S. A., 17 rue Lejeune, F–31000 Toulouse*

In Japan: Please write to *Penguin Books Japan, Ishikiribashi Building, 2–5–4, Suido, Bunkyo-ku, Tokyo 112*

In South Africa: Please write to *Longman Penguin Southern Africa (Pty) Ltd, Private Bag X08, Bertsham 2013*

READ MORE IN PENGUIN

LANGUAGE/LINGUISTICS

Sociolinguistics Peter Trudgill

Women speak 'better' English than men. The Eskimo language has several words for snow. 1001 factors influence the way we speak. Professor Trudgill draws on languages from Afrikaans to Yiddish to illuminate this fascinating topic and provide a painless introduction to sociolinguistics.

Bad Language Lars-Gunnar Andersson and Peter Trudgill

As this witty and incisive book makes clear, the prophets of gloom who claim that our language is getting worse are guided by emotion far more than by hard facts. The real truth, as Andersson and Trudgill illuminate in fascinating detail, is that change has always been inherent in language.

Multilingualism John Edwards

This superb survey explores all the contentious topics about language: links between gender and speech styles, and the attitudes, aptitudes and brains of bilinguals. In its wit, scholarship and rich supply of unusual facts, *Multilingualism* is a book of compelling interest to anyone who cares about the role of language in society.

Grammar Frank Palmer

In modern linguistics grammar means far more than cases, tenses and declensions – it means precise and scientific description of the structure of language. This concise guide takes the reader simply and clearly through the concepts of traditional grammar, morphology, sentence structure and transformational-generative grammar.

Longman Guide to English Usage
Sidney Greenbaum and Janet Whitcut

Containing 5000 entries compiled by leading authorities on modern English, this invaluable reference work clarifies every kind of usage problem, giving expert advice on points of grammar, meaning, style, spelling, pronunciation and punctuation.